Secrets of the Short Game

PHIL
MICKELSON

SECRETS
OF THE
SHORT GAME

WITH GUY YOCOM AND T. R. REINMAN

HARPER

An Imprint of HarperCollins Publishers

SECRETS OF THE SHORT GAME.
COPYRIGHT © 2009 BY PHIL MICKELSON

Printed in the United States of America

For information, address
HARPERCOLLINS PUBLISHERS
10 EAST 53RD STREET
NEW YORK, NY 10022

HarperCollins books may be purchased for educational,
business, or sales promotional use.

For information, please write:
SPECIAL MARKETS DEPARTMENT
HARPERCOLLINS PUBLISHERS
10 EAST 53RD STREET
NEW YORK, NY 10022

FIRST EDITION

Designed by Tim Oliver

Library of Congress Cataloging-in-Publication Data
has been applied for.

ISBN: 978-0-06-186092-8

09 10 11 12 13   /QW   10 9 8 7 6 5 4 3 2 1

To my parents, who made my life in golf possible,
and my wife and children, who make it worthwhile.

• • •

FOREWORD
by Phil Mickelson Sr.

IX

• • •

INTRODUCTION
by Phil Mickelson

XI

3

5 I

1 5 1

1 0 5

1 8 5

Contents

Foreword

WHEN I FIRST PUT A CLUB IN PHIL'S HANDS, the intent was not
to create the champion golfer you know today. He was not quite
two years old, and as with everything my wife, Mary, and I went on
to do with our children, the only goal was to introduce him to an
activity we could enjoy together as a family. There was no way to
predict he would one day master the game to the extent he has and
pass that knowledge along to others. Phil's accomplishments have
been thrilling for us and so, too, is the publication of this book.

Much of what I did to develop Phil's game as a young child,
I did using teaching principles I learned in college. As the avid
golfer in the family, I became Phil's instructor, and in those early
days I made some very fortunate choices in directing him that
generated enthusiasm and helped start him on the path to success. ›

I don't mind sharing a couple of those principles, for I believe they can be of value to everyone, even the grown-ups seeking to improve their scores by reading what Phil has to say about the short game.

• • •

FIRST AND FOREMOST, I WANTED to make the game fun. Golf is a very difficult game and can be very frustrating. When introducing Phil to golf, mainly in our backyard practice area, I would try to sense when he was at the absolute peak of his enjoyment, and at that point I always found a reason we had to quit. By always stopping on a high note, Phil became almost obsessed with playing golf and would take his golf club with him everywhere he went, even to bed. As you work on the things Phil teaches you in this book, I'd suggest you not turn the practice into drudgery by going at it for too long. Leave the practice area on a high note and reflect on what you've done well. There's an awful lot of information in these chapters, and although it's sure to help you improve immediately, don't try to learn it all at once.

That leads to my second bit of advice pertaining to quality vs. quantity. Phil was an inquisitive young golfer, especially when he entered his early teens. Although he practiced a great deal, there was a thoughtful element to the way he hit balls. Phil took his time and would often pause between practice balls, reflecting on how he could hit the shot to make the ball do something different. He didn't machine-gun those practice balls. He very much concentrated on how shots felt and considered how to make some fly higher or spin more than others. It was all about quality of practice, not quantity. He spent a lot of time hitting balls, but he had other activities, too, and he instinctively tried to derive as much good as possible from his practice time.

Phil was also fascinated by cause and effect. I like to think that one of my early lessons for him about golf being a game of opposites had something to do with that. I showed Phil how you have to hit down to make the ball go up and explained why swinging to the left will make the ball curve to the right. He always hit balls with the "why" of each one in mind. When we practiced together in our backyard, we would occasionally wind up playing "call shot," predicting in advance what type of shot one of us was going to play, and then trying to pull it off. That was enormously helpful, because it forced Phil (and me) to institute a plan for each shot. As you practice the chips, pitches, and sand shots Phil shows you, have a purpose in mind for each one. On one shot, it may be the hinge-and-hold technique Phil executes so well. On another, it may be how far you open the clubface. But if you hit shots haphazardly, you won't derive as much good from Phil's advice as you could otherwise.

Another aspect that will help you is the photographs of Phil demonstrating the different types of short-game shots. During those early backyard sessions, my main concern was safety. Phil

was still in diapers, and as I hit chips and pitches I'd keep him occupied with a few golf balls to play with. I wanted him in my field of vision at all times, so his safe spot was directly across from me. After almost six months of this, the day came when he got his first small, right-handed club. In preparation for his first swing we switched places. After guiding him into a few fundamentally correct positions—his feet lined up correctly, his hands positioned close together on the grip, and so on—I backed away and told him he could now hit the ball. Much to my surprise, Phil responded in an unusual way. He immediately went back to his spot, regripped the club left-handed, and made a great swing, hitting the ball with the back of the club. After repeating this a second time, I was so impressed with his left-handed swing I decided to change the club, not the swing. We went to the garage and carefully sawed off the back, giving it some loft, reshaped the old face, then refinished that little old wood club. It became his favorite toy, and today that very worn club mounted in Phil's trophy room brings back many fond memories. In this book, Phil's demonstrating his technique left-handed may be a big advantage for the reader. With the face-on photographs especially, you can really inspect your swing positions as though you were looking in a mirror.

• • •

I REALLY ENJOYED TEACHING PHIL what I could about the game over the years, taking care to stress the fundamentals and avoid making it too complicated. I suppose the strategy worked, because Phil progressed rapidly. He was a scratch golfer when he turned fourteen, and I felt I had taken him as far as my knowledge would allow. It was time to turn him over to a more competent, experienced instructor and for me to take a backseat. After that, I served as a second set of eyes, and when Phil's teacher wasn't handy, would comment only when Phil asked me to. Those early years I spent with Phil, along with his little brother, Tim, and, sister, Tina, were priceless. I learned a lot about golf and even more about being a father. Today I'm proud of Phil beyond words, in part because of the golfer he's become but even more because of the type of person he is. I hope you enjoy the book and the time you spend with Phil.

I'm proud to have helped lay a foundation for Phil's game and the wonderful instructional material he presents in the following pages. As an avid golfer still looking for ways to improve my own game, I'm hoping to learn a few things myself.

—PHIL MICKELSON SR.

Introduction

I HAD NOTHING BUT FUN IN MY BACKYARD and that's a big
reason for the success I've had throughout my career. My life in golf
was formed there, and that experience has been the basis for my
entire golf game, my instructional DVD, and this book.

When my dad built a chipping green in the backyard, I was eight
or nine years old, and until I could drive that was about the only
consistent access I had to golf. I would end up mowing the grass,
and because I worked on it, my desire was to have it look good. And
because of that, I would try not to take deep divots. I would brush
the grass. I would try to keep the leading edge consistent through
impact. I would have to be careful not to blade it off neighboring
homes, although I wasn't 100 percent successful at that. It all led to
me discovering the most effective, consistent, and best way to chip. ❯

I spent countless hours back there and that's where I became creative, going behind the olive tree or orange tree, or running the ball through the bunker, hitting shots out of the sand, all of these fun little shots. But after awhile new kinds of fun were needed. It's 41 yards from the corner nearest the house to the edge of the canyon just behind the green. Dad would pay a nickel for a hole in one, and I spent months trying to earn my college tuition that way. As a teenager, I started hitting balls over the house from the front yard to the green in back and a lot of those nickels went for window repairs to our house and the neighbors'.

Now, there are many different ways to learn and I was lucky. My parents supported my practicing and playing, so I had many days, probably adding up to solid years all told, to learn the short game on my own. But this book is an easy way to learn what I've learned so there's no wasted time for you. When you go out to the short game area, there's no reason you shouldn't work on the proper fundamentals and pick up the short game exponentially quicker than I did. I know that for most people practice is a drag. They wear themselves out ingraining bad habits, or learning ways to get by with what they've got. But we're not here just to get by. This book is designed to help you develop a world-class short game. More than 50 percent of all shots taken in a round are from inside 50 yards. It only makes sense to spend more time on the short game than on any other single facet of the game.

• • •

THERE ARE MANY PLAYERS WHO HAVE NOT been great ball strikers but have made a tremendous living playing golf. And there have been many players who stroke the ball incredibly well and haven't had a tremendous career because of their lack of a short game. It all comes down to getting the ball in the hole. This is the most critical element of the game.

The method I'm sharing here starts at the hole and works out. What I call the "hinge-and-hold" method, the basic, essential move in all shots from the green to 50 yards out, is easy to understand. We're going to talk about how to become efficient from three feet in and how to hit all kinds of approaches into that three-foot circle. When we can excel there, the game becomes so much easier than trying to hit to a four-inch cup.

• • •

THE FULL SWING HAS CHANGED over the years as technology has changed. To take advantage of stiffer shafts with less torque, we've developed a swing with a more upright finish. Think of players in the 1960s and '70s, having to sag their legs at impact and hold on to the swing in an effort to combat a hook because of whippier shafts. But the technique for chipping has not changed at all. Think of the famous pictures of Seve Ballesteros pitching from the car park at Royal Lytham & St. Annes when he

won the 1979 British Open. Or Tom Watson, chipping in from the greenside rough on 17 in the 1982 Pebble Beach U.S. Open. Or before them, Billy Casper laying up on the par 3 third hole at Winged Foot every day, making four pars and winning the 1959 U.S. Open. Their wrists cocked on the takeaway, they accelerated through the ball, the clubhead never passed their hands at impact, and they maintained that angle in the follow-through. They didn't use this clock method or the "no-wrist" move that's being taught today. They used the hinge-and-hold, just like every good short game player has used and continues to use.

We'll take a look at what's happening on the greens, how to read them, how much a putt is actually breaking, and how to become a great putter. The perception has been that you're innately a good putter or you're not. I say that's not so. Touch, feel, reading greens, all of it can be easily learned given the proper instruction and technique. Years ago, Dave Pelz ran the World Putting Championship. It was open to everyone from severely handicapped people to tour pros and the results showed anybody can putt and putt well. You can learn to putt, you can learn to chip, and you can be as good or better than a pro in those areas.

• • •

I'LL TRY TO SHY AWAY FROM THE OBVIOUS, how a chip breaks like a putt or breaks less when you fly it in the air. I'm assuming you have a basic understanding of the game. The goal of this book is to take your game to the top level from 50 yards in, giving you an understanding of the short game and a foundation for great technique—identifying the problems and giving you the solutions.

But let's not forget the fun of it. When I go out with my daughter, Sophia, we almost always finish with a putting contest. Maybe I have to give her a couple of strokes for the five or six holes we play, but we have a competitive match; she two- and three-putts very nearly every time. She's become a good putter, and she looks forward to our matches.

I'm hoping you'll enjoy this experience, too. Enjoy learning an effective new technique. Enjoy working at it and seeing dramatic improvement in your short game. Enjoy posting lower scores. And have more fun playing golf than you've ever had before.

—PHIL MICKELSON

"The type of stroke you use is almost irrelevant. What's important is that you return your hands and the clubface to the same positions they were in at address."

I

Reading greens well is both a science
and an art. Never hit a putt until you have
a clear perception of speed and line.

→ SECTION I

Putting

I'D HAD TO MAKE PUTTS BEFORE, especially in the previous hour, but I really needed to make this one. I'd dreamt about winning the Masters since I was a child. I'd prepared for it since I first played Augusta National in 1991 and had come close, with three consecutive third-place finishes. But close doesn't count when you're chasing your dream, especially one this big. Ernie Els was on the practice green behind me, waiting to see if I settled for par. If I did, we'd go to the 10th tee for a sudden death playoff. I had to make this putt right now. ›

THERE ARE FOUR KEYS TO good putting: read, speed, alignment, and stroke. You have to make a good read on the green–see the break between your ball and the hole and adjust your line accordingly. You have to have good pace on the ball–a feel for the speed of the green along your line. You have to be aligned correctly, both vertically–head, shoulders, waist, and feet–and horizontally–along your intended line. And you have to put a good stroke on the ball–the face angle at impact must be correct. You may have read the line correctly, hit the ball with the right pace, and you may be perfectly lined up. But unless you hit it squarely on your intended line, the putt is not going in. Once you have those four keys in place and start making putts, your confidence will soar.

• • •

WHEN I WAS IN COLLEGE I would bang everything at the hole and more often than not bang in just about everything that missed long. That worked for me on greens that weren't nearly as quick or against competition that wasn't nearly as stiff as on the PGA Tour. In my first PGA Championship,

at Inverness in 1993, I was paired with Ernie Els and, for the first time in a tournament, Jack Nicklaus. For two days I marveled at Jack's ability to get long putts close. It was clear that I had to change my style; I had to improve my lag putting to take the pressure off having to make the short misses or comebackers for par.

I worked on that and did improve quickly, but I really made a jump when I began working with Dave Pelz in 2004. One of the things we identified was my need to get my putts started squarely on line more consistently. Together, we created a training device called The Putting Tutor. A spot to place the ball is on one end of a triangular piece of plastic. At the other end is a "gate," two small metal balls set just wider apart than the width of a golf ball. We set the Tutor on the correct line and then practice stroking the ball through the gate. If you can stroke the ball correctly on line for the first 10 inches through the gate, with the right pace, you're pretty much assured of holding the line all the way to the hole.

• • •

AS I STOOD ON THE 12TH TEE in the 2004 Masters, Ernie was making eagle on the 13th hole to take a three-stroke lead. He

wasn't finished and I had to start. I made a 12-foot birdie on 12, a two-putt birdie on 13, another from about a foot on 14, and after a 15-footer on 16, I was tied for the lead.

My approach on 18 stopped about 18 feet above the hole, just in front of Chris DiMarco's ball, which meant I was going to get a good read on the pace and line. That was a good break. I thought about Payne Stewart one-putting five of the last seven holes at Pinehurst in the U.S. Open five years earlier, and the confidence he showed on the 18-footer he made for the win. My own confidence level was soaring–as I'd made four birdies in the last six holes. It was a good feeling. But as I approached the putt, I left that trance and went back into my Putting Tutor mode. I aimed for a spot just left of the line Chris had taken on his putt, which had narrowly missed, took two practice strokes visualizing the gate in front of my ball, and then stepped in and stroked it into the hole. Working at it, believing in my practice routine, and making the biggest putt of my life meant my dream had come true.

Treat every putt the same regardless of pressure. Your preshot routine and the rhythm of your stroke never change.

→ SHAPING YOUR STROKE

ONE OF THE FIRST "RULES" OF PUTTING I heard was that the putter should travel along a straight-back, straight-through path, with the face of the putter aimed at the target at all times. That may be true, but then again it may not be. The path of your stroke, and how much the clubhead rotates while you swing the putter, depends on the type of putter you've chosen. The idea is to let the basic design of the putter determine the shape of your stroke for you. If you fight the putter's behavior as determined by its design, you're really fighting physics—and that's a battle you won't win. There's an endless array of putting styles, with plenty of room for individual nuances. But you should use a putter that matches up with the stroke that feels best.

→ **LET THE PUTTER DECIDE ARC**

The path of the center-shafted putter (A) is straight back and through, with the clubface staying square from start to finish. Conversely, the heel-shafted model (B) produces a curved arc, in part to accommodate the natural opening and closing of the clubface. I like the heel-shafted model and the stroke it encourages, but it's strictly a matter of personal preference.

CHOOSING A PERFECT MODEL

The key difference in the two putters at right is not the shape of the clubheads, but the point where the shaft enters the clubhead. A center-shafted model (A) has no tendency to fan open and closed during the stroke. A heel-shafted model (B) will rotate freely, because the clubhead tends to revolve around the axis where the shaft joins the clubhead.

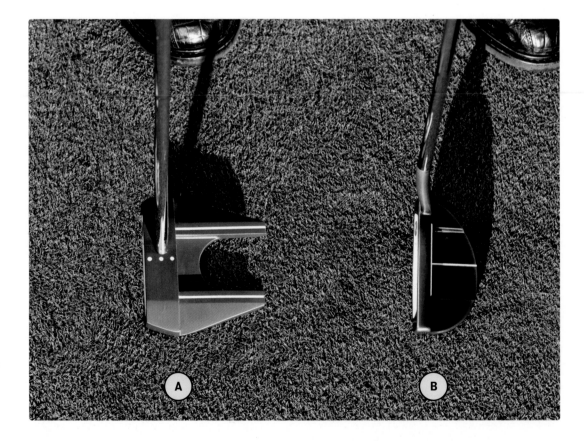

A

B

→ SETUP & GRIP

YOUR BODY POSITION at address should be predicated on feeling relaxed and comfortable. There are a few mechanical considerations but not many. My main goal is to feel a sense of softness in my arms, hands, legs, and torso. My stance is no wider than if I were standing talking to someone, and I bend at the waist in such a way that my back doesn't feel rigid or tense. My arms hang easily, with no conscious straightening or bending. Because the putting stroke is a relatively small motion, the purpose of the setup is to set the stage for a rhythmic motion that is smooth but precise.

SETUP IS THE SAME, EVERY SINGLE TIME

My putting setup doesn't have much nuance to it. What I do pride myself on is consistency. I follow a routine that puts me in the exact same position on every putt. When my setup is complete, you can't tell if I'm addressing a 40-footer or a 3-footer.

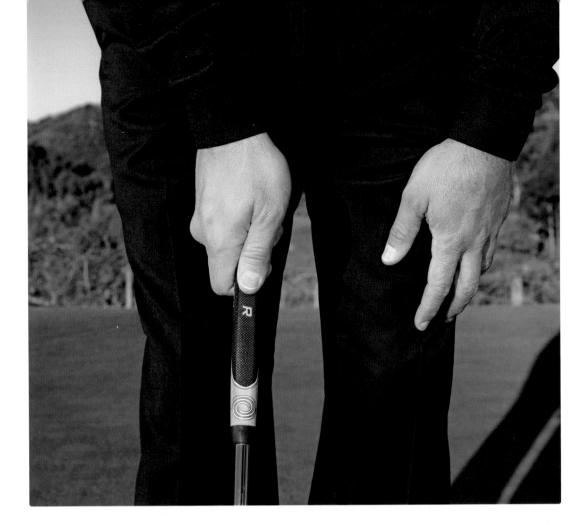

ESTABLISH A "STRONG" TOP-HAND GRIP

Because my putting stroke involves some rotation of the clubhead and a "release" on the forward stroke, it's important that the top hand (the one uppermost on the grip) be in a position to turn. Place your top hand on the grip (*top*) so you can see two knuckles when you look down at address.

Next, simply add your bottom hand, with the palm facing the target (*below*). The thumbs of both hands should be positioned on the flat portion of the grip, to enhance your feel of the club. Note how the index finger of my top hand lays atop the fingers of my bottom hand. That nuance gives a sense of unification, the two hands performing as a unit during the stroke.

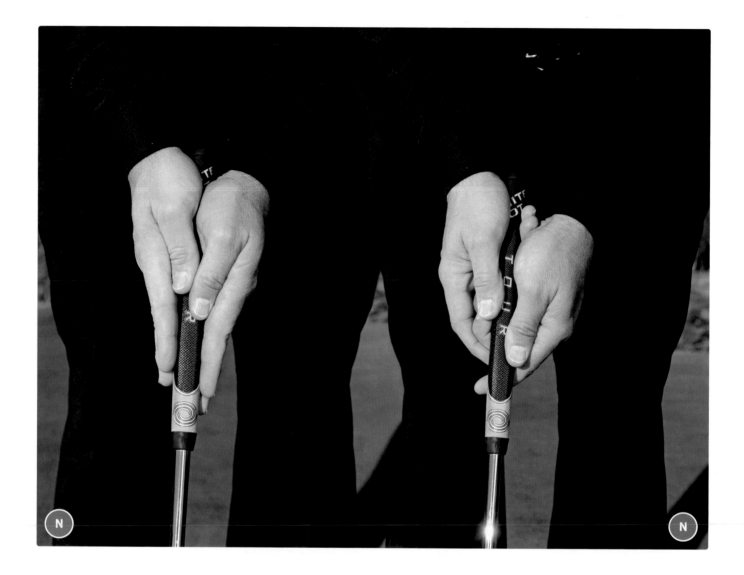

→ EXPLODING A MYTH

GOLF IS FILLED WITH TEACHING AXIOMS. Many are very sound, while some leave a lot to be desired. A good example of a poor putting axiom is the "hands opposing" philosophy. The idea (it is said) is to have the palms of the hands opposing each other when you complete the grip, so you can keep the clubface square to the target line from beginning to end. I believe the palms-opposing method does more harm than good. It immobilizes your hands and undermines your ability to swing the putter freely. It makes it difficult to open and close the clubface naturally, which is especially important on longer putts. The method also limits your touch and feel, and in general is a style you should ignore if you want to become a good putter.

NEVER LOCK YOUR HANDS

Here's the palms-opposing method in action. When you close your hands on the putter, your wrists are unable to hinge and both hands are discouraged from rotating. This type of grip is designed to take the hands out of the stroke, and certainly it does that—there's no way you can exert good touch and feel with this type of grip.

SOFTNESS AND SENSITIVITY ARE YOUR GOALS

I can't emphasize enough the importance of holding the putter softly and keeping your grip pressure light at all times. You should hold the putter firmly enough to have control, but never to the extent where you're consciously squeezing it.

If you watch me on the greens during tournaments, you'll note that I establish my top-hand grip first, then add my lower hand very gently (*left*). You'll see me opening and closing my hands around the putter a couple of times, until they are knitted together just right (*inset*). It's mostly feel-based, and the finished product looks—and feels—comfortable and relaxed.

→ BALL POSITION

WHERE YOU PLACE THE BALL
in relation to your stance at address
should above all be consistent. Some
players prefer the ball at the center of
their stance, a few like it well forward,
and most (myself included) prefer it to
be just forward of center. Whatever your
preference, the important thing is to
position the ball exactly the same every
time. There are two reasons for this: first
because of its effect on clubface loft;
second, because it determines where
along the swing path you make contact.
Keep in mind, inconsistent ball position
will result in a poor, inefficient roll, and
lots of pulled and pushed putts. Since
my ball position falls in line with the
accepted norm among good putters,
I strongly suggest you copy it and make
it part of your routine.

PLAY BALL SLIGHTLY FORWARD IN YOUR STANCE

This is the ball position preferred by most good putters, and for good reason. My eyes are positioned farther down the target line, or "behind" the ball, giving me a clear view of both the ball and hole. That helps my aim. Because my hands are positioned forward (toward the target) at address and at impact, the clubface has just the right amount of loft when I make contact, and the clubhead moves slightly on the upswing.

With the ball a bit forward, it gives more time to square up the face of the putter at impact and avoid pushing the putt off line. Another secret to avoiding the push is to use a heel-shafted putter similar to mine, which tends to rotate more easily into a square position at impact.

If you position the ball in the middle or rear of your stance (*top inset*), you'll tend to deloft the clubface and hit down abruptly, causing the ball to jump and roll poorly. If it's too far forward (*bottom inset*), you'll add loft and get the ball airborne instead of rolling it smoothly along the green from the start. In both cases, the chances of you pulling or pushing the putt are magnified due to your making contact with the ball too early or late as the putter travels along its arc.

→ HOW FAR FROM THE BALL SHOULD YOU STAND?

A SECOND ELEMENT OF BALL position concerns how far from the ball you stand at address. In our earlier discussion on basic models of putters, I explained how a center-shafted putter tends not to twist during the stroke due to the axis being located in the center of the clubhead. In addition to resisting twisting, the center-shafted model performs best when it travels on a straight path, both away from the ball and swinging through. You want to promote that path, and the simplest way to do it is to stand fairly close to the ball at address, with your eyes directly over the ball (*near right*). Remember, you want to stand this close only when you're using a center-shafted, fairly upright putter.

A HEEL-SHAFTED PUTTER MEANS MORE DISTANCE FROM BALL

Because I prefer a heel-shafted putter, it follows that I want to stand farther from the ball at address than if I were using a center-shafted model. In the photo at near left, you'll note that my eyes are slightly inside the target line. As I move farther from the ball, the path of my putter becomes curved, with the putter traveling inside the target line on the backswing. It moves back onto the target line through impact, but then travels back inside the line on the follow-through. The face of the putter also tends to open and close, much like a door swinging on its hinges.

TWO MODELS, TWO SWING PATHS

The center-shafted putter (A) requires that you stand closer to the ball than with a heel-shafted model (B). If you've ever watched players who use the extra-long putter—the type anchored high on the chest—you'll notice they always stand very close to the ball. The main reason for that is the design of the clubhead—they are always center-shafted models. Consequently, their swing paths are straight back and through.

With my eyes behind the ball, I can observe all three of the elements that matter: the ball, the path to the hole, and the hole itself. The view is similar to crouching behind the ball during the initial read, but the benefit here is having my eyes parallel to the target line.

→ LIKE AIMING A RIFLE

A SLIGHTLY FORWARD BALL

position helps you see the line better and assists you in aligning your body and aiming the clubface. If you watch me in tournaments, you'll frequently see me in the position you see in the photo at near right. After I've gotten a general read of the putt, I'll emulate my position at address, albeit more bent over with my eyes nearer the ball and putting surface. What I'm doing is sighting the ball, line, and hole together, in much the same manner one would aim a rifle by looking down the length of the barrel. It gives me a full perspective that wouldn't be possible if my eyes were directly over the ball; it would be like placing my eyes at the far end of the rifle barrel.

PART ONE OF A TWO-STEP TEST

Stand at address and place a second ball near the bridge of your nose. Drop the ball and note where it lands. It should make contact well to the rear of the ball you're addressing.

PART TWO: BALL LANDS "INSIDE" LINE

To make sure my eyes are slightly inside the target line (due to the heel-shafted putter), I repeat the ball-drop test. It should land nearer my feet than the ball I'm addressing.

→ UNDERSTANDING LOFT

PUTTERS ARE SOMETIMES thought to be the one club in the bag with no loft on the clubface. It's not true, of course. Although the purpose of the putter is to propel the ball forward along the green, it does have loft– 4 degrees in most cases, though top players often customize their putters to have a bit more or less. Ideally, you want to get the ball airborne to the extent it can skim along the top of the grass briefly before gravity and friction cause it to start turning end over end. For that to happen efficiently, you want the putter to have the same amount of loft at impact as you established at address.

NOT A FLAT-FACED CLUB

As you can see in the photograph at right, the face of my putter has enough loft to avoid driving the ball into the putting surface at impact. On the other hand, I don't want so much loft that the ball sails through the air with a lot of backspin and bounces unpredictably when it returns to the ground.

ANATOMY OF A PERFECT ROLL

Having become airborne immediately after impact, the ball in the photo above is in the process of skidding. After it travels another inch or so, it will begin rolling smoothly in a nice end-over-end manner. Check out the putter, too. It's suspended off the surface of the green, because it has passed the lowest point of its arc. Finally, notice that the face of the putter is square. I've hit this putt very solidly, and there's a good chance the ball found the center of the cup.

→ DANGER OF DELOFTING

THERE ARE MANY WAYS TO MISS A PUTT. You can misread the line, aim the putter poorly, make poor contact, or hit the putt with too much or too little speed. But one of the most common problems is a flaw within the stroke itself. I'm talking about delofting the putter, either by placing your hands too far forward at address, or shoving them forward during the stroke. In both cases you drive the ball downward into the green, causing it to bounce and then roll very unpredictably. The biggest casualty is speed; the ball will roll too far or come up short. But starting the ball on the correct line is an issue, too, because there's no telling for sure which direction the ball will travel when it rebounds off the green.

HOP, SKIP, AND A NASTY JUMP

The shaft of my putter is leaning well toward the target (*below*), the first sign I've delofted the putter. The second sign is the clubface, which has no effective loft at all. But the most important feature is the ball itself. It's a good quarter-inch off the ground, the result of the putter driving it into the surface of the green at impact. The ball has rebounded, and where it will go is anybody's guess.

SHAFT LEANING WELL FORWARD SIGNALS TROUBLE

When you lean the shaft too far forward at address or through impact, you deloft the face of the putter to the extent that it has negative loft—it's actually tilted downward into the surface of the green. But pushing your hands forward during the stroke has another dangerous consequence: It tends to open the clubface (*left*). This usually results in a pushed putt. If you compensate by rotating your hands excessively, it can mean a pull.

→ NEVER ADD LOFT

INCREASING CLUBFACE LOFT is even more common than delofting. It happens either by placing your hands too far behind the ball at address, or by unhinging your wrists and allowing the clubhead to pass your hands through impact. Either way, the clubface has more loft than intended and the outcome is poor—even worse than delofting in most cases. When you add loft, the ball jumps into the air and acquires backspin. The quality of contact is usually poor as well, due to you making contact on the bottom part of the clubface. One way to address the problem is to use a putter that has almost no loft to begin with. But it's far better to improve your stroke.

A RECIPE FOR INCONSISTENCY

The close-up photo above reveals that the shaft of the club is leaning backward, meaning that the clubhead has passed the hands. The ball is off the ground by a good half an inch, and there's no telling how it will react after it lands. One thing is for sure: By adding loft you're not imparting a smooth, true roll, and will never be consistent from day to day.

WHEN A PUTTER BECOMES AN IRON

A standard, off-the-rack putter has 4 degrees of loft. When you allow the putter to pass your hands, you basically are adding several degrees of loft—enough to transform the putter into an iron. The effect on the ball's behavior is only part of the problem. In the photo at left, I'm pointing to the leading edge of the clubface, where impact typically occurs. Hitting putts "thin" causes some serious issues with speed, because you aren't hitting the ball solidly. After coming up short a few times, the tendency is to give your stroke a little extra pop. The sudden acceleration with your hands is no good, either.

The forward press can help trigger the takeaway and sets the stage for your hands moving toward the target later in the stroke. It is not a dramatic motion. After you complete your setup and address (grip, stance, aim, and alignment), your hands will be directly over the ball (*near right*). At that point, all you do is nudge your hands a few inches up the target line (*far right*). When you complete the forward press, you are modeling the position you will be in when the putter makes contact with the ball.

→ SHOULD YOU FORWARD PRESS?

ALTHOUGH THE PUTTING STROKE doesn't have a large range of motion, it does require rhythm. Because you're motionless as you stand over the ball at address, you need some sort of signal to set the club into motion. Some players simply do it mentally, beginning the stroke when they sense they are ready. Others, myself included, use a forward press– a slight forward movement of the hands that precedes the club moving away from the ball. Whether or not you use a forward press is a matter of personal preference, but if you adopt it, you need to make sure you don't change the aim of your clubface.

→ # HANDS NEVER PASS CLUBHEAD

YOUR HANDS LEAD THE WAY on every stroke in golf. It's a rule that is no less important in putting than any other area of the game. When your hands pass the clubhead and make an angle between your front arm and the clubshaft (*shown near right*), it results in all kinds of problems. You're adding loft to the clubface and causing the clubhead to move faster than your hands—a big mistake. You get a poor roll with poor speed and, with that combination, you can't accomplish anything.

HANDS ALWAYS KEEP MOVING

Two features of the stroke I'm making in the photo at near left aren't especially dramatic to look at, but they are extremely important to every good putter. First, my arms and the putter are moving at the same speed, with my hands leading the way and moving straight toward the target after impact. This helps me accelerate the putter smoothly, keep the clubface square, and control the speed of the ball. Second, I haven't allowed my wrists to unhinge in the slightest. My arms and hands are behaving as a unit and accelerating up the line. As a general rule, don't accelerate the putter abruptly by releasing the clubhead with your hands. If you do, you'll add loft to the clubface and have huge problems controlling speed.

→ A WORLD THREE FEET IN DIAMETER

ON THE MAJORITY OF SHOTS FROM 50 YARDS AND IN, your goal should be to get the ball within three feet of the hole. That's the magic number, because from three feet and closer I make 97 percent of my putts. As you move farther away the chances of making the putt decrease exponentially. From four feet I make 90 percent of my tries and from five feet only 75 percent. From six feet the percentage plummets to 55 percent! Strategically, then, you not only want to get within three feet, you then want to ensure that you very rarely miss putts from short range. A drill I learned from Jackie Burke, the legendary player and putting expert, has made holing short putts a cinch. It's so effective, I've made it part of my everyday practice and warm-up routine.

When you begin the three-foot circle drill (*opposite right*), you want to establish a sense of rhythm right away. Move smoothly from one ball to the next, counting each putt silently as it drops. One...two...three and so on, interrupting the process only to retrieve the balls and reset the station once you've filled the hole. Think of making short, crisp strokes, giving each putt the proper pace. Continue...25...26...27... You'll notice that the pressure increases as you get closer to your target figure. That's good. That's when you learn to build trust in your stroke.

THE 100-BALL PRACTICE DRILL

Place a series of 10 tees in the ground, each three feet from the hole. Repeat, but with the tees stationed in concentric circles four, five, and six feet away. Place balls next to the tees of the innermost circle, and see how many you can make in succession. My goal is 100 straight. Your target figure should match your skill level. If you miss, start over!

→ THE 2005 PGA
CHAMPIONSHIP:
PRACTICE PAYS

I CAME to the last
hole of the 2005 PGA
Championship at
Baltusrol tied for the
lead. Needing a birdie to
win, I hit my second shot
on the par 5 hole short
and left of the green.
When my pitch stopped
three feet from the hole,
I raised my arms in
the air. I wasn't taking
victory for granted, but I
just knew the three-
footer for birdie would
drop, because I had hit
thousands of them before
while performing the
three-foot circle drill.

When it was my
turn, I stood away
from the ball, making
practice strokes (A). I
was counting to myself,
85...86...87, as though
I were going through
the drill. To this day
I do this often. When
finally I stepped in and
addressed the ball (B), I
felt almost no pressure at
all. I tricked myself into
viewing it as just another
putt in the drill.

The putt to win
my second major
championship was 88!

→ NOW WIDEN YOUR
PRACTICE CIRCLE

AS YOU MOVE FARTHER FROM THE HOLE, you begin confronting some challenging new features. Whereas the three-foot putts had very little break and you had some margin for error in terms of speed, the four-, five- and six-foot ranges really start bringing those factors into play. In the photo above, I'm at the six-foot range and have started paying attention to speed and break, which change considerably as I progress around the circle. I concentrate less on rhythm and more on observing the line, speed, and break as I approach each ball. The drill is essentially the same, but by placing more emphasis on speed and break, I get a good feel for how the greens are rolling.

FEWER "MAKES," BETTER READS

Since a sand wedge is typically 36 inches long, two club lengths will give you the six-foot distance you're looking for. When you begin moving around the circle, the first thing you'll notice is that not many putts are dropping. That's OK; measure your success by how well you anticipate the speed and break of each putt, which will vary a lot from ball to ball.

ON SHORTER PUTTS, USE THE 25/75 EQUATION

From six feet and in, you need a short, controlled backswing. A long backswing won't work consistently, as you'll either decelerate the putter on the way to the ball or risk hitting it too hard if you catch it solidly. I like to think "25/75," meaning that if you measure the length of the stroke from start to finish, the backswing constitutes 25 percent of the distance (A), while the follow-through consumes 75 percent (B). This will promote a firm, decisive stroke that is easy to control. The clubface doesn't have room to open or close excessively, and you'll accelerate the putter through the ball. Remember, keep your grip pressure light.

A

B

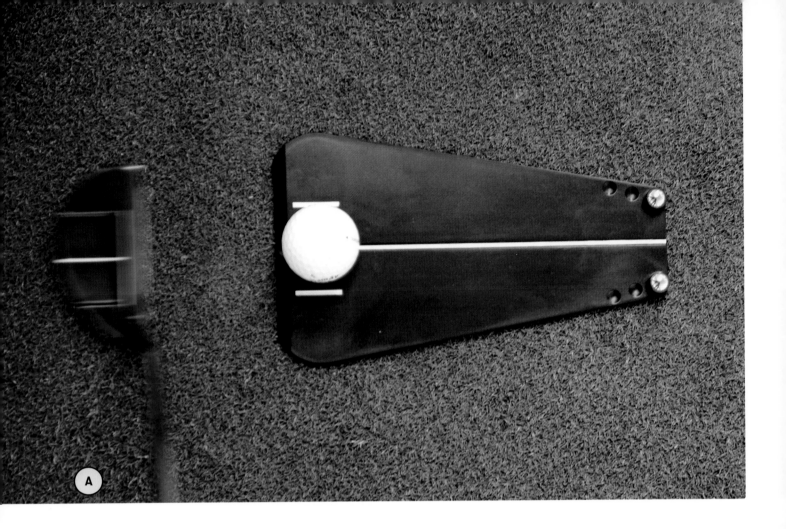

A

→ THE IMPORTANCE OF AIM (AND A DEVICE TO HELP)

CLUBFACE ALIGNMENT MAY BE THE MOST CRITICAL ELEMENT OF putting. You can make a beautiful stroke, but if the face isn't aimed correctly you're guaranteed to start the putt to the left or right of your intended line. Conversely, if the face is aimed well, you can make a poor stroke and still have a reasonable chance of holing the putt. Aiming the face accurately has been very challenging until now, because golfers have had to depend on their eyes alone—a guessing game, really. The Putting Tutor training device, developed by Dave Pelz and me, fixes this problem once and for all. I use it every time I practice, including at Augusta National while I prepare for the Masters. It teaches proper aim, green reading, speed control, and starting the ball on line.

A DAUNTING CHALLENGE

The Putting Tutor features two small lines that bracket the ball, a sight line that extends down the line of play, and two free metal balls you place in one of three sets of holes near the end of the device (A). The holes nearest the ball are wide apart and are for those struggling with face aim. The holes become progressively narrower. You're looking here at the "pro" setting.

(B)

(C)

A LESSON IN AIM AND ALIGNMENT

I like what I see in (B), and not just because the ball is about to pass through the "pro" setting gate without knocking either of the metal balls out of their holes. Notice how the sight line on top of my putter isn't quite parallel with the corresponding line on The Putting Tutor. This proves I've "released" the putter, or allowed it to rotate slightly closed after I've contacted the ball—a function of my heel-shafted putter. At impact a moment earlier, the face was dead square. The face continues to rotate well after the ball is gone (C), further proof I've held the putter lightly and released it freely.

PERFECT PRACTICE

→ ADD THE TUTOR TO YOUR ARSENAL

The Putting Tutor is the best practice putting device on the market today. It is available for $49.95 and can be purchased through Dave Pelz's Web site at pelzgolf.com.

<figure>/ 33 /</figure>

→ LET'S TAKE A LESSON

USING THE PUTTING TUTOR
in the sequence of photos at right, I'm demonstrating how all the components of putting come together. The string represents the line of play. The sight line of The Putting Tutor is aimed down that line. As you can see, I'm playing about two feet of break. The white dots depict the path the ball will follow en route to the hole. Alignment, aim, speed, and break are all factors here. The most important aspect is how the ball began falling toward the hole almost immediately after I made contact. When you factor in speed and break while reading the green, do it with the understanding that the ball will begin losing momentum immediately after it is struck. The ball's apex, or the point where it begins "taking the break," is defined by the moment after impact, not later, as many players assume.

(A)

MAKE AIMING SECOND NATURE

I've started the ball on the correct line (A), because the clubface is aimed perfectly. Train your eyes to register what the correct putter aim looks like so you can do it automatically on the golf course.

REMEMBER THE BASICS

The principles I stressed earlier—hands leading the clubhead and moving down the target line after impact—are apparent here (B). Don't let your hands or the putter "cheat" toward the hole!

BALL BREAKS MORE AS SPEED DECREASES

Given a steady, consistent side slope, the ball will break most dramatically as it slows near the end of its roll (C). Consider that when you determine the line and envision the ball's path to the hole.

→ THE NO. 1 TYPE OF MISREAD

I'VE NEVER MET AN AMATEUR who played enough break on putts of 20 feet or longer. Research has shown that every single amateur–and many pros–see less break than is actually the case. Thus, they can hole the putt only if they (1) hit the ball extra hard (which decreases how much the ball will curve); (2) misalign the putter so it's inadvertently aimed "correctly"; or (3) make a poor stroke, pulling or pushing the putt so it starts on the true line. The problem obviously lies with the inability to read greens correctly, but it also ties in with aiming the putter accurately and hitting the ball with the right speed. In the photos at right, I demonstrate what happens when you make a good stroke, but misread the line.

NO CHANCE FROM THE START

The string is aligned roughly eight inches outside the cup (A), while the tee represents the true line. I've started the ball on the string, but it's well below the white dots signifying the correct path.

GOOD SPEED AND AIM, POOR LINE

At this point, it's obvious the ball is going to miss on the low side of the hole, even though I've aimed the clubface well and started the ball on the intended line (B and inset). I just didn't play enough break.

THE ROOT CAUSE OF THE MISS

Most amateurs would reflexively think they had pushed this putt, and consequently blame their aim or the stroke. In truth, my aim was excellent (inset). I simply failed to aim far enough outside the hole.

→ SUCCESS BY ACCIDENT

UNDER-READING PUTTS is a chronic problem, but one amateurs don't diagnose very well. They rarely correct the problem on their own, because they hole just enough midrange putts to convince themselves they're doing something right. In truth, the only time they make the putt is when they do something wrong–pull or push the putt above the line by accident. It's a case of two wrongs (poor green reading and inaccurate clubface alignment) making a right. This is where The Putting Tutor is invaluable, because it reveals indisputably the correct line, and it helps you straighten out your aim and stroke at the same time.

(A)

POOR AIM, GOOD RESULT

I'm playing only eight inches of break, as indicated by the string (A). Note that the ball is starting well outside the string. It's going toward the tee in the ground–the correct line, as it turns out.

CROSSING OVER

For the ball to find its way onto the correct path (B) as indicated by the white dots, it has to cross under the string. At this moment, most amateurs feel they've started the ball on the line they saw at the outset. Not the case!

BEATING A BAD HABIT

When you see a putt like this one drop (C), the excitement and satisfaction tricks you into thinking you read the putt correctly. There's one solution to this problem: Practice your green reading as diligently as you do your stroke and aim.

→ LAGGING THEM CLOSE

THE GOAL FOR PUTTS OUTSIDE 40 feet is to get the ball within three feet of the hole, where we know the second putt will drop. Speed control is pretty delicate, which is why players three-putt downhill putts much more often than when they're putting uphill. On lag putts we're obviously hitting the ball with greater speed than from short range. You do that by varying the length of your stroke, not by applying a sudden burst of energy when you begin the forward stroke.

I've developed a very helpful practice routine that will improve your touch and ability to regulate the length of your stroke. I started using it two months prior to the 2006 Masters, and it went a long way in helping me win my second green jacket. It's called the 40-50-60 drill, and you begin by stationing three balls at increments of 40, 50, and 60 feet from the hole. Place tees in a three-foot circle around the hole, to help you define your goal.

A

STEP 1:
START AT 50 FEET

Start at 50 feet. Keeping
your grip pressure
as light as possible,
make a long, flowing
stroke, imparting as
much rhythm as you
can. On your next two
tries, concentrate on
adjusting the length of
your stroke to roll the
ball the correct distance.

C

STEP 3:
THE 60-FOOTER

At the far extreme is the
60-foot lag. You have to
strike each of the three
balls emphatically to
get them close, and the
key is to control your
rate of acceleration.
Make a longer backswing
and then apply the same
amount of energy as you
did on the shorter lags.
Allow the longer stroke
to generate the speed
you need to reach the
three-foot circle.

STEP 2:
MOVE UP TO 40 FEET

Next up is the 40-foot
station. The slightly
shorter stroke should
give you a feeling of
more control. The rate
of acceleration on
the forward stroke is
the same as for the
50-footer, but the putter
is traveling a bit more
slowly because the club
didn't travel as far on
the backswing.

→ THE "MONEY" BALL

ALWAYS WRAP UP THE 40-50-60 drill with one final, meaningful effort. After I hit three putts from each of the three distances, I move back to the 50-foot increment and hit a 10th putt. On this putt, it's like I'm a kid again imagining I need two putts to win the Masters or U.S. Open. Mentally, I take myself out of practice mode and put some real pressure on myself. I also put something material at stake: If I don't get the ball within the three-foot circle, I have to start the entire 40-50-60 drill over again. This sharpens my intent and concentration, and makes me focus on *exactly* how long a stroke I need to make to get within the three-foot circle.

ONE LAST TRY, DO OR DIE

When you putt the 50-foot money ball (*right*), go through your entire putting routine. Read the green as though you were playing from this spot for the first time. Make purposeful practice strokes, envisioning the exact length of backswing needed to get the ball inside the circle. And I'll say it one last time: Hold the putter as lightly as you can while still maintaining control.

/ *Phil's philosophy* / "When you're practicing long lags, don't limit yourself to putts across a flat portion of the green. To get a true feel for distance, practice uphill and downhill lags as well."

KEYS TO A GREAT LAG STROKE

There are two variables in your stroke: The length of the stroke and the energy you apply on the forward swing. Your goal is to make one of those variables—the energy you apply swinging the putter into the ball—the same every time. The length of the stroke will vary depending on the distance of the putt, the speed of the greens, and whether you're putting uphill or downhill, but the rate of acceleration you apply never changes. In the photos above, I've accelerated the putter smoothly through the ball, letting it gather speed gradually (*left*). The putter continued through impact into the full follow-through you see here (*right*).

→ LESSONS
IN ACTION

›

In reading this putt, I'm focusing on the few feet of fairway the ball needs to cross before reaching the green. My main concern is speed. Obviously I'll need to stroke the putt more firmly than if I were on the green, but just how firmly depends on the height and moisture of the grass, as well as the "grain"—the direction the grass is growing.

‹

For me, reading greens is a team effort. My caddie, Jim (Bones) Mackay has been with me virtually my entire career, and we speak the same language when it comes to putting. When Bones gives his input, he does so knowing how hard I like to hit the ball. If you team with the same partner in weekend matches, it pays to read greens the same way.

›

Judging by the length of my follow-through and how far the putter has come off the ground, the putt I'm stroking here is a long one. On lag putts I concentrate hard on letting the putter gather speed steadily on the forward stroke. The speed the putter is moving at impact is determined by the length of the backswing.

‹

I've just holed a six-foot putt for par to win the 2009 Northern Trust Open by one shot, and what a feeling it was! The putting keys I've presented in this section are ones that will work under pressure. In fact, the more pressure, the better it works. One of the best feelings in golf is standing over an important putt just *knowing* it's going to drop. If you practice the technique I've shown, you'll experience that feeling often.

"The ideal chipping stroke is one that is aggressive yet doesn't cause the ball to fly too far or run long. By adjusting your ball and clubface position and length of your swing, you can play every type of chip in the book."

49

→ SECTION II
Chipping

WINNING THE CA CHAMPIONSHIP at Doral in March 2009 was tremendously satisfying for me for a couple of reasons. Five years earlier I had led the same tournament for the first three rounds but lost that lead on the 71st hole. I needed a chip from near the grandstands downhill to the back-left pin on 18 to get into a playoff; it lipped out. So to see a putt from pretty much the same line cozy down to tap-in range for the 2009 win was sweet. But more important, I got confirmation that my short game was as good as ever, if not better. ›

I WAS COMING OFF A BAD double bogey in the first round when my approach to the par 3 fourth hole bounced off the bank right of the green and into the water. I had an uphill lie to the hole, which was cut on a downslope running away from me. That meant I had to get the ball up quickly but somehow make it land softly enough to avoid it running long and leaving me with a long par putt—and possibly a second straight double bogey. I struck the ball crisply; it checked on the green and then released, rolling slowly into the hole to save a crucial par. That sudden change of momentum helped me birdie the next hole to get back to par for the round. I birdied five of the next 11 after that one.

By the time I got to the 17th hole, I was near the lead. But my approach finished in fluffy grass just left of the green. I was left with a delicate chip from about 25 feet above the hole. I had to hit that shot about 10 feet to get it rolling slowly toward the cup. The ball popped over the deep stuff, nicked the collar with just enough spin, and edged into the hole for a birdie. I would have

been delighted with a simple par.

After a great drive on the dangerous 18th my approach came up just short of the green, about 35 feet from the hole. This called for a very different shot from the last two. This one was straight uphill and into the grain. Now it wasn't a matter of trying to get it to slow down, but of getting it to release and run up the hill. It did, and my third chip-in birdie of the day gave me a share of the lead I held through all four rounds.

• • •

THOUGH EACH SHOT LOOKED different—uphill to a downslope pin, downhill to a short pin, uphill and into the grain—each was executed with the same hinge-and-hold method. There were subtle adjustments made for each shot—the wedge I used, ball position, angle of attack, club-face position—but one constant was a controlled yet aggressive move through the hitting area. On the first shot, the ball was slightly forward in my stance, and the face was open to help get it up quickly. On the second, it was pretty much in the middle of my stance, because it only needed to hop a few feet, a distance easily covered thanks to the natural loft of the club. On the third, the ball was slightly back

in my stance, which de-lofted the club and promoted a lower trajectory and a run to the hole.

• • •

I HAD TO GET UP AND DOWN quite a bit at Riviera earlier in the year, where the greens are smaller than at Doral, and I was successful enough to win there, too. Once I got to Doral, I fully realized that my short game had improved fairly dramatically over the off-season—in large part because of the work I put into writing this book and creating a DVD. I had worked on the scoring shots around the green since I was a kid in my backyard, and it had become sort of automatic for me. Now I really thought hard about what I was doing technically so I could articulate it for readers and viewers, and that mental review brought my game into sharper focus for me. The hinge-and-hold method, the ball position, and seeing the line and the speed weren't done just through memory anymore; they were alive and well in my conscious thinking.

Longer chips require a more aggressive swing, and a longer follow-through.

→ ONE WEDGE IS SUFFICIENT

AS A KID, I PRACTICED CHIPPING ENDLESSLY IN MY BACKYARD. I'd hit all kinds of shots, and when it came time to practice hitting the ball low, I was reluctant to break up my session and retrieve my 9-iron from the garage. Instead, I found ways to hit the ball low with the club I had—an ordinary sand wedge. To this day, I use just one of my two 60-degree wedges (the one at right in the photo below), for virtually all chips and pitches, controlling trajectory by altering my ball position or adjusting how open or closed the clubface is at address. This runs contrary to the strategy used by many top players and the multiclub philosophy recommended by teachers. But I like using that one club. I'm familiar with its weight, how it looks when I set it down at address, and how the ball reacts when I make contact. I believe it's the most dependable way to approach the short game, and I strongly recommend you give it a try.

WEDGES: TAKE YOUR PICK

Both wedges pictured below have 60 degrees of loft, but they are markedly different. When I rotate the wedges to an open position, the construction of the sole on the left club raises the leading edge off the ground considerably. The bounce has increased, making it good for some sand shots. For chips and pitches, I prefer the wedge on the right, as the leading edge stays the same height off the ground regardless of how far I open the face.

KNOW HOW YOUR WEDGE WORKS

The ideal specs of your wedge are largely about personal preference. But I personally feel that a fairly wide sole (*right, above*) is helpful on shots where you deliberately want to hit slightly behind the ball. You also want a wedge where the leading edge sits a little off the ground, even when the clubface is set square at address (*left*).

→ SIMPLIFY YOUR SETUP

MY SETUP HAS BECOME second nature to me. After so many years playing the game, I rarely give it a second thought. That should be your goal—flowing into your address position instinctively, without thinking about mechanics. Your setup should be more sensory-oriented than technical, with a big emphasis on feel. I don't think about the technical aspects of the grip (whether it's strong or weak, or where my Vs should point, for example) as much as how lightly I'm holding the club. A similar rule applies to my stance and posture. I pay more attention to making sure my body feels relaxed than I do making everything textbook perfect. Because the chipping motion is so small, you don't need to prepare your body to make a lot of movement.

BASIC CHIP: NOTHING FANCY

Chip shots are largely feel-oriented. To heighten your sense of touch, hold the club very lightly and form a narrow stance, with your feet fairly close together. Make sure your upper back, arms, and hands are relaxed, and that you have no tension in your legs. The softer you keep your entire body, the better your rhythm, tempo, and feel will be when you execute the swing.

PREP FOR SUCCESS

It's important that no part of your setup become stiff and mechanical. Let your arms hang naturally so you aren't reaching for the ball at address. Make sure you bend forward just enough to create room for your arms to move away freely on the backswing (*left*). Hold the club slightly more firmly than you do your putter. You want your wrists to feel loose so they can hinge easily on the backswing (*inset*). If you obey these feel-oriented principles, you'll address the ball consistently, with no conscious thought.

→ THE BASIC MOTION

EVERY SHOT FROM 50 YARDS IN IS PLAYED using the same method. I call it hinge and hold, and it applies to chips, pitches, sand shots, flops, and lobs. I hinge and hold often, because it's the cornerstone of my short game. The beauty of it is, it doesn't take exceptional talent to execute it well. It's simple, easy to perform, and can be learned quickly.

    The essence of the hinge and hold is this: You hinge your wrists early in the backswing, while limiting how far back you swing your arms. On the downswing, you simply maintain the hinge in your wrists and accelerate through the ball using your arms. There is no "release" as most people describe it. You don't deliberately throw the clubhead into the ball. The hands always lead the way on the downswing, with the club trailing behind. In addition to deliberately keeping the hinge in your wrists intact, you also curb rotation in your hands. The clubface stays square through impact, ensuring that the ball starts on the correct line.

HINGE WRISTS
ON TAKEAWAY

The first move back is a smooth cocking of your wrists. On short chips, your hands don't move away from the ball (*above*), and your arms stay very quiet. Keep your grip pressure light, so you cock your wrists smoothly, with good rhythm. Never snatch the club away from the ball.

SHOT DISTANCE DETERMINES SWING LENGTH

Never swing your lead arm very far back, even on longer chips or those requiring more height and greater clubhead speed. You vary clubhead speed by how much you hinge your wrists. In the photos at left, I'm playing two types of shots. In the top photo, I'm playing a long chip with a low trajectory, while in the bottom photo I'm playing a shot that is 15 yards longer and that determines a higher trajectory—and needs more clubhead speed. Notice that my arm swing on the longer shot is only fractionally longer than on the shorter shot, while the amount of wrist break has increased dramatically.

→ HOLD THROUGH IMPACT

THE ROOT CAUSE OF MANY SHORT-GAME PROBLEMS is giving in to the impulse to release the clubhead by unhinging the wrists on the downswing. It's caused by anxiety, a feeling that you must somehow help the ball into the air or otherwise hurry the clubhead into the ball. In truth, there is only one correct way to perform the downswing, and that's by maintaining the hinge in your wrists. If you keep your wrist cocked and simply accelerate your arms forward, all kinds of good things happen. At impact you'll preserve the amount of clubface loft you established at address. You'll acclerate into the ball and control your distance better. You'll hit the ball cleanly rather than thin or fat. Your rhythm and tempo will be smooth, which in turn improves your sense of feel. Finally, you'll deliver the clubhead into the ball on the proper angle, neither too steep nor too shallow. Learn to trust this method and use it on every shot–it's the only way to play.

HANDS AND ARMS LEAD, CLUB FOLLOWS

You can maintain your wrist hinge through impact without fear that you'll deloft the club and fail to get airborne sufficiently. In fact, keeping your wrists hinged will actually produce *more* height than releasing the club, because you won't hit the ball thin. Lead with your hands, the clubhead trailing behind (*below*), and trust in the loft of your sand wedge to produce the elevation you need.

/ *Phil's philosophy* / "The shaft of the club leans slightly toward the target at impact. A helpful thought is to maintain the same target-leaning shaft angle several inches into the follow-through."

CLUBHEAD NEVER PASSES HANDS

Even on the follow-through, the back of my leading hand doesn't buckle outward. The label on my glove faces the target, not the ground. That's a sign that I've maintained the hinge in my wrists and refused to let the clubhead pass my hands. Notice how the clubshaft and my leading arm (*above*) form a straight line, another sign my hands have led the way.

→ ERROR NO. 1: HANDS PASS

I BELIEVE IN EMPHASIZING THE RIGHT THINGS TO DO in the swing rather than what you should *not* do, but some errors are so common and have such a disastrous effect on the swing that they are worth bringing to your attention. If you catch yourself making these mistakes, you need to take action right away. None of the other principles of good chipping can take effect unless you correct these basic errors.

The first error I see is allowing the clubhead to pass the hands. If your handicap is in the mid- to high-double-digit range, it's almost certain you're making this mistake—and not only in your short game. Allowing the clubhead to pass your hands by unhinging your wrists will wreck your full swing, too. If this mistake is part of your makeup as a golfer, the good shots you hit will happen by accident rather than by design.

The stiff-wristed, arms-only backswings I'm demonstrating at right will cause you to come into the ball on a shallow angle, bringing the leading edge into play and causing lots of thin, skulled chips. You also can err the other way, hitting the ground behind the ball. The clubhead then bounces off the turf and into the ball—another skulled shot. At best, this so-called clock method results in poor touch and distance control.

→ ERROR NO. 2: THE "CLOCK" FALLACY

I'VE HEARD TEACHERS SAY the backswing and follow-through should be the same length. They reference a clockface and suggest the chipping swing go from, say, 4 o'clock on the backswing to 8 o'clock on the follow-through. There are a few problems with this philosophy. First, it encourages an arms-only backswing, with no emphasis on hinging the wrists. Second, it leads to a shallow angle of approach into impact, with the club moving parallel to the ground instead of downward into the ball. Third, the clock method instills tension in the arms and hands as you try to make them behave as a unit back and through. The motion looks stiff and manufactured, with no flow at all. It really leads to problems when you get into the longer chips, where hinging the wrists becomes necessary for purposes of speed alone. The clock method just doesn't work and should be erased from the teaching playbook.

→ **THIN, BUT NOT TO WIN**

The contact you make with the clock method is rarely solid. It feels and sounds clunky because you're hitting the ball thin, and the ball behaves erratically, with different amounts of spin from shot to shot. Invariably the follow-through is too long (*inset*) relative to your follow-through, and the entire method causes you to grip the club too tightly with stiff, rigid arms devoid of feel.

→ ALWAYS ACCELERATE!

TO MAKE THE HINGE-AND-HOLD TECHNIQUE WORK effectively, your arms and hands must accelerate steadily throughout the downswing. They are actually traveling fastest just after impact. When you watch slow-motion replays of top players chipping, you'll notice that their arms and hands travel farther on the follow-through than they did on the backswing. Acceleration and momentum are the cause of that, and they are necessary on every chip. If your hands move decisively through the ball, with the clubhead lagging behind, you ensure that the clubhead approaches the ball at the proper angle and catches the ball flush. The clubface will be square at impact, guaranteeing that you start the ball on the correct line. And the clubface loft you established at address will be exactly the same at impact, so the ball leaves the club at the height you saw in your mind's eye when you planned the shot.

ACCELERATE HANDS, NOT THE CLUBHEAD

It's important that you apply acceleration with your arms and hands. It's also important not to try to speed up the clubhead by unhinging your wrists. Think of the club as an extension of your arms and hands, and make them behave as a single, unbroken unit. Where the arms and hands go, the club will follow. A good thought is to never allow the club to move faster than your arms. You control speed and distance by how fast you accelerate your arms and hands into the follow-through (*right*).

HANDS MOVE TOWARD TARGET

An image that will help you accelerate is to visualize a line running from the ball to the target. On the forward swing, your hands move directly up that line and don't stop until the ball is well on its way to the flagstick. This image promotes accuracy, too—if you keep your hands moving up the target line, the clubhead will move up the target line as well.

→ CHIP OPTION NO. 1

THE TERM "SHOTMAKING" usually applies to the full swing, but it applies to the short game, too. I'm always pleased when people compliment me on my imagination around the greens. The source of that is my willingness to try different types of shots from the same location. The most obvious example of short-game shotmaking is in the way I play the short chip from a good lie. One option (albeit one I don't use very often) is with my 9-iron. It's one of the very rare instances when I don't choose my 60-degree wedge, but it comes in handy when I want the ball to roll immediately after it hits the green, with as little checking action as possible. It's a good choice when I'm chipping uphill to a green that slopes severely from back to front.

PLAY BALL FORWARD IN STANCE

Using my 9-iron (*right*), I don't need to make any special adjustments to hit the ball low. The clubface has only 42 degrees of loft (much less than my 60-degree wedge), so I don't need to play the ball back in my stance or lean the shaft forward dramatically to get a low trajectory. Nor do I need to strike the ball as firmly as I would my wedge.

LESS LOFT EQUALS SMALLER MOTION

My backswing with the 9-iron is short, with not much wrist break and no swinging of my arms at all (*inset*). I keep the clubhead fairly low to the ground, so my angle of approach into the ball is shallow, almost like a putt. The downswing is simple and deliberate, without much force. All I do is move my hands toward the target and allow the clubhead to stay low to the ground into the follow-through (*left*). The ball doesn't come off with much backspin, due to the lack of loft and clubhead speed. The ball begins rolling almost immediately after landing on the green.

→ CHIP OPTION NO. 2

FROM THE SAME LOCATION and lie, I am now using my 60-degree wedge. All things being equal, I prefer to play the shot with the wedge, as it gives me more versatility with spin and trajectory. This option is definitely better when I have a decent amount of green to work with and the shot is downhill, because the shot lands more softly with some added bite. My setup differs from that with my 9-iron in one way: I play the ball much farther back in my stance, opposite the toe of my rear foot. That effectively reduces the loft of my 60-degree wedge so the ball comes out only slightly higher than with my 9-iron, but with much more spin. Notice that my hands appear to be farther forward than on the 9-iron chip, but my hand position is about the same. It's an illusion created by the shaft leaning toward the target.

SETUP DETERMINES SHAPE OF SWING

By moving the ball back in my stance (*right*), I've programmed a steep backswing followed by a sharp downward blow into the ball. Changing ball position and club selection will influence the behavior of the club and the outcome of the shot without having to consciously alter the shape of the swing. It's an efficient way to create shots.

WHEN YOU NEED A LITTLE "BITE"

My ball position has led to a steep angle of approach and a clean hit. Because my lie was good, with the ball sitting up, I was able to strike the ball first and then allow the clubhead to continue down, taking a nice little divot (*left*). The steep angle of approach helps the grooves on the clubface grab the ball and create a lot of backspin, even though I didn't swing with a lot of speed. The ball is coming out low, and after it hits the green it will take a couple of bounces and then check before rolling toward the hole. Notice that my hands continue forward after impact (*inset*). Although I hit down sharply, I'm still hitting through the ball, not at it.

→ PRACTICE YOUR TRAJECTORY

DEVELOPING A GOOD SHORT GAME
obviously requires practice—the right kind of practice. The biggest obstacle to improving isn't necessarily how much time you spend hitting shots from around the green; it's the quality of that time. Most amateurs assume that if they put in enough time and sheer effort, a payoff is waiting on the other end. That isn't always true. If you work on the wrong things and don't add variety to your practice, your progress will pretty much be frozen. The smart way to practice is to vary your trajectory. If you can consistently control how high the ball flies by changing your ball position, clubface position, and club selection, your improvement will be genuine and permanent. Never hit the same shot more than a few times in a row. Free up your imagination and mix up your distances and trajectory. It makes practice fun and stimulating, and you'll have a greater command of different shots when you get out on the course.

WHEN TO COME IN HIGH

As a rule of thumb, you want to hit the ball high (*top*) when (1) you don't have much green to work with; (2) the green is very firm and fast and you need the ball to settle quickly after landing; or (3) you're playing to an elevated green. To hit the ball high, your lie has to be reasonably good. With practice, you can learn to hit the ball high from tall grass and bare lies—later on I'll show you how—but for the most part you want the ball sitting up so you can make clean club-ball contact.

WHEN TO COME IN LOW

Chipping the ball low (*bottom*) is usually the safer, easier play with more margin for error. Go with the low chip when (1) you have a lot of green to work with; (2) the ball is sitting down or in an otherwise poor lie; or (3) you're playing to the upper tier of a two-tiered green. When you practice, alternate between playing the low shot and the high one—and try a few that are in between!

STEP 1: SET UP SQUARE

Start by aligning everything—the clubface, your stance and shoulders—square to the target at address (A). It's important that you learn to set up square to the target accurately without thinking about it, so it helps to lay a club along your feet, running parallel to the target line. Also, ask a friend to double-check that the leading edge of the clubface is aimed true.

→ A FOOLPROOF WAY TO CONTROL HEIGHT

YOU KNOW BY NOW THAT hitting the ball high requires that you open the clubface at address. But if you've simply been opening the clubface and making no other adjustments, chances are you're inconsistent in terms of height, direction, and making solid contact. You probably find yourself manufacturing an unusual and uncomfortable type of swing to get a decent result. In fact, opening the clubface correctly involves adjusting your grip, stance, and body positions. When done well, hitting the ball extra high gives the impression the player is blessed with great hands and sense of timing. Adjusting your shot height appears difficult, but that just isn't the case. Whether you're hitting an extra-high chip shot or a full-blown flop, it's strictly a matter of following a simple procedure before you set the club into motion. The execution part is easy.

A

(B)

STEP 2: OPEN THE CLUBFACE

With your stance remaining square, open the clubface (B). How much you open it depends on the distance of the shot and how high you intend to hit it. For now, open it so that when you look down, the leading edge is aligned at about 2 o'clock on an imaginary clock face (10 o'clock if you're a lefty like me).

The next stage of the process is to gradually rotate your stance open until the clubface is aligned squarely at the target. Don't just rotate your feet. Allow your shoulders to open along with your feet so everything is aligned away from the target. As you go through the procedure, make sure you don't shift your hands in any way. Notice that my grip remains unchanged from what I had at address **(C)**.

C

→ OPEN BODY AS WELL AS CLUBFACE

WITH THE CLUBFACE NOW OPEN to the target line, many amateurs stop right there and swing away. That's no good, because the clubface is aimed well away from the target and you need to conjure an unnatural out-to-in swing path to hit the ball high and straight. Cutting across the ball makes it difficult to hit the ball solidly, because the clubhead is

D

**STEP 4: REGRIP
THE CLUB**

The last check before
beginning the downswing
is to regrip the club (D).
As you go through the
entire procedure, it's easy
to make the mistake of
twisting your hands to
manipulate the clubface.
It makes the opening of
the clubface artificial,
because during the
downswing your hands
tend to return to the
position they were in
at address. Until the
procedure becomes
second nature, it's a good
idea to regrip the club.
This will guarantee that
the clubface is open in
relation to your feet and
shoulders, but square to
the target when the setup
procedure is complete.

approaching the ball on too steep an angle. You're also leading
with the hosel of the clubhead, which leads to the possibility
of a disastrous shank. Finally, it's difficult to maintain the open
clubface to the exact degree you established at address. What
you need is a couple of additional adjustments that allow you
to add sufficient loft, while not swinging out to in.

→ PUTTING THE PIECES TOGETHER

THE FOUR-STEP PROCEDURE will, with practice, flow together smoothly, with no interruption. Just as there's a rhythm to swinging the club, preparing to play a shot should have a nice, even pace to it. When you hear a PGA Tour player say, "I had a nice rhythm going," he's talking as much about the smoothness of his preshot preparation and the way he moved between shots as he is about the way he swung the club. Certainly I feel that way when I'm playing well.

As you practice putting together the four-step procedure, learn to do it as briskly and seamlessly as possible so it comes naturally when you begin using it on the course. The key is to form a clear mental picture of the shot you want to hit before you begin the process. That way, you can begin the procedure decisively with clear intent. If you feel a twinge of doubt during any segment of the process, simply back away and start over. It's better to be safe than sorry.

PRACTICE WITH THE GOAL IN MIND

The purpose of the four-step procedure isn't simply to open the clubface at address. The reason you aim the clubface at the target (top) and then rotate it open (center) is so it will be open during impact. If you fan the clubface closed through impact, your good work will come undone. On the other hand, if you preserve the loft you established (bottom), the ball can't help but come off with the trajectory you programmed.

FINALLY, FIRE AWAY

Now you're ready for the payoff. Once the process is complete, make your normal swing using the hinge-and-hold technique. Do not alter your swing by cutting across the ball from out to in, swinging extra hard, or trying to help the ball into the air. Keeping your grip pressure soft, accelerate your arms and hands directly up the target line (*left*), maintaining the hinge in your wrists. Make sure the clubface doesn't rotate closed; you'll ruin the loft you established earlier and the shot will come off too low. I think you'll be amazed at how quickly you progress with this procedure. Before long, you'll have excellent control over the ball's trajectory, how far it flies, and how it behaves after it lands on the green.

→ THE HIGH, SOFT CHIP

ONE OF THE MOST IMPRESSIVE SHOTS in the tour pro's arsenal is the chip that attains a great deal of height despite the player using a short swing. It doesn't seem possible, at first glance, that the player can hit the ball so high using a swing that imparts so little clubhead speed. It's impressive on another count as well. It's obvious the player has to make very precise contact and hit the ball solidly, which is quite a feat considering the clubface is laid open. If you don't catch the ball exactly on the sweet spot of the clubface, you won't apply enough energy to make the ball pop high into the air, and the shot will come up short. Nevertheless, it's a shot you can learn to play, and it's vital that you add it to your repertoire. It's a very valuable tool when you're chipping to a downslope or you don't have much green to work with.

A REAL TEST FOR AMATEURS

When you're chipping to a fast, firm green that is running away from you (*right*), it's important to land the ball on a precise spot on the green. The ball must also touch down at a steep, near-vertical angle to avoid having it run past the hole. You're controlling distance not by backspin—the shot is too short to apply very much of it—but by trajectory. It takes a soft, accurate touch and good technique to pull it off.

ADJUST YOUR BACKSWING TO MATCH THE SHOT

As on all shots, it's important that you accelerate through impact. The length of your backswing is critical here. Too long, and you'll decelerate and flub the shot, leaving it short of the green. Too short, and you're prone to rushing the downswing and stabbing at the ball—another recipe for disaster. You want to program the shot carefully, with an open clubface. And you want to make sure you're "measured off" correctly at address (*inset*) so you can count on solid contact. You must also find the right length of backswing (*left*) so you achieve proper acceleration.

MAKE A FIRM, AGGRESSIVE DOWNSWING

To get the ball up quickly, you must program plenty of clubface loft at address. Opening the clubface sufficiently frees you up to make a firm, accelerating downswing without fear of propelling the ball forward on a flat trajectory. You'll get plenty of ball speed, but the ball will fly with a steep trajectory. In fact, the ball will travel a greater distance vertically (*right*) than it does going forward. Keep in mind, this is not a flop shot. You're making a shorter backswing and follow-through than on the flop shot, and you're hitting the ball solidly rather than delivering a glancing blow.

→ "TRAPPING" VERSUS "SLIDING"

ON ANY GOLF SHOT, ALL THAT REALLY MATTERS is impact. As I take you through the different short-game shots, you'll notice I place tremendous emphasis on how the clubhead should move through impact, and why. There's a lot of variation in the type of impact conditions you want in chipping, pitching, and in the flop and lob. But in chipping, your objective should always be the same: a "trapping" condition at impact. On the

**TURF MAY SHORTEN
YOUR FINISH**

Although you're hitting
the ball high, you're not
taking it to extremes as
you would with a flop or
lob, or even a longer pitch
shot. You aren't trying
to spin the ball furiously
or make it fly 30 feet
in the air. You want a
short, crisp, fairly steep
downswing in which the
clubhead meets some
resistance from the turf.
Sometimes this will give
you a shorter finish,
sometimes not. In the
photo at left I've clearly
accelerated through the
ball, but the modest
swing speed combined
with my clubhead being
slowed by the grass kept
my follow-through from
being too long. Notice
how my hands have led
the way, and how I've
kept the clubface open.
The result is a shot that
lands on the green in
a "dead" fashion, the
downslope of the green
carrying the ball toward
the hole.

high, soft chip, you want to compress the ball a bit, with the
grooves on the clubface grabbing the cover of the ball. It's why
I like to see the clubhead descend on a slightly steep angle and
accelerate through the ball. There are shots where we "slide"
the clubhead under the ball and intentionally make less than
perfect contact. On this shot, though, you want the quality
impact that comes from the trapping action I described.

→ THE LOW, RUNNING CHIP SHOT

IF YOU HAVE PLENTY OF GREEN to work with, the low chip that runs a good distance after landing is almost always preferable to the high, soft chip. The main reason is safety. The low chip has a much greater margin for error, because it requires a smaller swing and is easier to strike solidly. You play the ball farther back in your stance, which makes it much easier to hit crisply than when you position it farther forward. There also is the fact that you deloft the clubface by setting your hands well ahead of the ball and align the clubface squarely at the target—factors that, again, make the shot more forgiving on slight mishits. Then there's the fact that the ball behaves more predictably when it hits the green. The low, running shot is much easier to start on the correct line and is less likely to bounce off line if it hits some imperfection on the green. The low shot is a safe, dependable play.

LOW SHOT DECREASES THE RISK

The situation at right is similar to the one where I played the high, soft chip. So long as the ball has room to run out, the low chip is usually the better option. In the photo at right, the ball has landed just beyond the fringe and is rolling the rest of the way to the hole. The shot will have more backspin than the high chip and will check after landing, preventing it from running over the green.

BALL BACK, FACE SQUARE

In some ways, the low chip is similar to a putt. You align the leading edge of the clubface directly at the target line, and you position the ball farther back in your stance (*inset*) than for a standard chip or pitch. Of the two main aspects of the chipping equation—distance and direction—the direction part is easily solved, making the low shot a good choice when you don't need the ball to stop quickly after landing on the green.

PLANNING A STEEP DESCENT

Because the ball is farther back in your stance than on a standard chip, your normal swing will create a steeper backswing (*left*) and sharper angle of approach into the ball on the downswing. My swing may appear long, but it's almost all wrists—I'm barely moving my arms. Thus, I'm assured of generating a good amount of speed, but not so much that that I risk hammering the ball past the hole.

THE LOW RUNNER

→ CONTROL THE ANGLE OF ATTACK

A STEEP ANGLE OF APPROACH

really pays off on this shot. You can tell I've made clean contact and really pinched the ball off the turf, and it's the sharp downward blow that made it possible. Although the ball is coming out low, it's loaded with backspin. Now, if my lie were poor, with the ball nestled in taller grass, the steep angle of approach would work even more to my advantage. The grass would prevent the ball from spinning as much, but the sharp angle of descent still would enable me to make decent contact. Good lie or bad, a decisive downward blow gives you better control over distance and direction. As long as you keep the leading edge of the clubface aimed down the target line through impact and beyond, it's easy to predict how the ball will react.

ACCELERATE, EVEN ON SHORTER SHOTS

This shot is not a long one and requires even less speed than I applied on the high chip. Still, my rule about always accelerating into the finish (right) remains intact. Keep your hands moving forward!

THE CLUBHEAD TRAILS AT FINISH

Keeping your hands ahead of the clubhead at all times is always important, but that rule is especially true when you're hitting the ball low (*above*). In addition to keeping the loft of the clubface low, it encourages solid contact and makes it much easier to hit the ball on line. With my follow-through complete and the ball slowing as it rolls toward the hole (*left*), I'm waiting for the ball to break toward the hole and finish within the three-foot circle.

→ DEALING WITH BAD LIES

BAD LIES ARE A FACT OF LIFE IN GOLF. Most shots that miss the green result in a less than perfect lie and many of them put you to the test as a golfer. The problem with bad lies around the green is they limit your ability to control the ball. When your ball is sitting down in tall grass, you're lucky to apply any backspin at all, and controlling distance and trajectory becomes a real problem. I've been playing golf for close to 35 years, but even with practice and the experience I've gained, I still find my ball in lies where I'm just not sure how the ball is going to react. I've learned to accept the reality of bad lies and accept the limitations they impose on my game. By constantly trying new techniques—the most valuable of which I'll demonstrate here—and improving my strategy, I've reached a point where I frequently save par, and when that isn't possible, at least hit a decent enough recovery. As a result, the bad lie rarely costs me more than one stroke.

NOT THE NIGHTMARE IT SEEMS

Pictured below is the classic bad lie, the ball sitting down in thick rough. How the ball reacts when you play from a lie like this depends on the thickness and moisture of the grass, how deeply the ball actually is resting, and the quality of your contact. One thing's for sure: Although the lie is difficult, you definitely can learn to play the shot well enough to have a reasonable chance at getting up and down.

OPEN CLUBFACE IS A MUST

Your first inclination upon seeing your ball in tall greenside rough may be to dig it out using the sharp leading edge of the clubface. In truth, you'll have much more control and a better result if you open the clubface at address (*left* and *inset*). You're going to want to hit this shot with some force in order to penetrate the grass, and only if the clubface is open can you do that without hitting the ball too far. In addition to creating extra loft, you're exposing the sole of the club rather than the leading edge, which helps prevent the clubhead from getting snagged in the grass through impact. An open clubface is a must on this shot.

THE BAD LIE

→ LEAN FORWARD, HIT DOWN

THE TECHNIQUE FOR THIS SHOT is somewhat similar to playing the buried lie in sand. The idea is to expend the force of the swing downward so the clubhead plows under the ball and forces it up and out onto the green. You should intentionally try to hit a few inches behind the ball; if you strike too close to the ball it's anybody's guess how the ball will come out. Like the buried lie in sand, you want to set the stage for the sharp downward blow by leaning your upper body toward the target with most of your weight on your front foot. Remember to open the clubface. You're going to need a lot of loft, both to get the ball airborne and to free you up to apply a lot of speed through impact. You can't baby the shot or get too cute with it; your best chance is to go after it aggressively.

A

ACTIVATE YOUR ARMS AND WRISTS

Notice that my arms have swung back a healthy distance for a shot of this length (A). Unlike the standard chip, you can't rely solely on hinging your wrists to generate speed. Swing your arms and, if necessary, turn your shoulders.

B

C

ELEVATION IS NOT A PROBLEM

Because you're leaning toward the target and keeping your weight on your front foot (B), your backswing and downswing are quite steep. Firm up your grip and swing down forcefully behind the ball, and it will pop up nicely.

DOWNWARD HIT MEANS SHORT FINISH

If you hit down sharply as you should, the angle of descent combined with resistance from the turf will result in a short follow-through. Still, I've managed to extend my arms (C), a sign that I accelerated into the grass behind the ball.

→ THE FLUFFY LIE

SOMETIMES THE BALL DOESN'T SETTLE DEEPLY in the rough. Quite often the ball will be suspended midway between the top of the grass and the ground beneath it. For inexperienced players, it's a tricky lie. They aren't sure whether to pick it cleanly or play it as though it were sitting down severely. What they learn is picking it cleanly results in a thin or topped shot, while trying to explode the ball out results in the clubhead passing so deeply underneath the ball that they hardly make contact at all and fluff the shot so badly it doesn't reach the green. The fluffy lie is actually an easy shot to play, and you shouldn't have much trouble getting the ball within the three-foot circle and consequently a successful up and down. As bad lies go, this one is pretty forgiving; you can hit the ball slightly thin or heavy and still get a good result. Just make sure it's a fluffy lie and not a truly bad one—lean down and inspect the lie before you play the shot.

SQUARE THE CLUBFACE AT ADDRESS

From the fluffy lie, square up the clubface (*below*) so it's aimed at the target. Unlike a poor lie with the ball sitting down, you don't *need* or *want* an open clubface (*inset*). You're going to swing through the ball in a sweeping manner, and since there isn't enough grass behind the ball to grab the clubhead and slow it down, you can feel confident about exposing the leading edge of the clubface.

You'll want to swing
through the ball on a
shallow, sweeping angle,
the clubhead traveling
almost parallel to the
turf. To that end,
you want to level out
your setup at address
so your weight is
distributed evenly on
both feet. Position the
ball a bit forward of
center in your stance,
so your backswing
and downswing are
discouraged from
getting too steep. Make
sure your entire body is
relaxed. There is no
need to hold the club any
more firmly than usual.
A nice, soft grip pressure
will improve your feel
and give you better
distance control.

THE FLUFFY LIE

→ FLAT PLANE PROMOTES SOLID HIT

THE SWING FROM A FLUFFY LIE IS slightly different than for standard chips and pitches. Instead of cocking the club upward to program a fairly steep angle of attack on the downswing, the fluffy lie requires a swing plane that is decidedly on the flat side. If you compare the sequence of photos at right with other shots I've demonstrated, you'll notice I'm swinging more around my body, with my hands traveling well inside the line of play on the backswing. A flat backswing promotes a downswing that is more shallow, with the clubhead traveling fairly level through the hitting area. The hinge-and-hold method is still intact, but I'm hinging my wrists less and swinging my arms more. The action is smooth and rhythmic, with a milder rate of acceleration through the ball. Try to keep your head and upper body still and your lower body quiet. You don't need a lot of clubhead speed, due to the club being delofted, but you do need to remain steady to help promote solid club-ball contact.

A

SWING AROUND RATHER THAN UP

If you look at my clubshaft on the backswing, you'll notice it is flatter in relation to the horizon than on other shots (A). That sets up a sweeping-type action through impact, the clubface meeting the ball in a head-on manner.

SWING THROUGH THE BALL, NOT AT IT

Look carefully at the divot I'm taking (B). The clubhead hasn't penetrated down far enough to reach the dirt under the grass. My level angle of approach has shredded the grass behind the ball, but it hasn't disturbed the roots.

PLAN FOR A MIDRANGE TRAJECTORY

The ball flight isn't particularly high, but neither is it low. Although the clubface was square at address, the loft of the 60-degree wedge is still sufficient to get nice height. Plan for a shot that is 50 percent carry and 50 percent roll.

If you've tried putting
from off the green but
aren't satisfied with your
performance, chances
are you're focusing
on the green rather than
the fairway. The fact
that the green is much
faster than the fairway
instills a fear of hitting
the ball too hard and
having it run too far after
it reaches the putting
surface. When you size
up the situation, focus
on the fairway and how
much speed you need to
apply so the ball rolls at
the right pace when it
reaches the green. If the
fairway slopes one way
or the other, keep in mind
that much of the break
will be negated due to
how hard you hit the
ball. A fast-rolling putt
will steam through
a mild slope without
breaking much.

→ PUTTING FROM OFF THE GREEN

PRIOR TO MY FIRST MASTERS TOURNAMENT WIN in 2004, I
made several changes in my approach to playing the course
that helped enormously. An important one was my shot selection around the greens. For years I had chosen to employ
standard chips and even flop shots. But the tight, "sticky" lies
you get around the greens at Augusta gave me little margin for
error, and on several occasions I paid a heavy price. So, when

Be careful about adjusting your setup or stroke to accommodate the slower speed of the fairway. After you've gained some experience, you can try placing your hands farther back at address (which adds loft to the putter) and other little shotmaking tricks, but at the outset you should stick with a conventional setup and stroke. One more tip: Use your putter only if the ball is sitting up and you can make clean contact. If your lie is poor or if there's an obstacle directly in front of your ball—an old divot, perhaps—then leave the putter in your bag and go with your wedge.

the opportunity presented itself, I began using my putter. The greenside grass at Augusta is mowed very short—about the height of greens on a municipal course—and I found it easy to roll the ball close to the hole for some easy pars. Since then, I've often used my putter from off the green, including a couple of key shots during my 2009 CA Championship victory at Doral. It's an easy, low-risk shot.

LESSONS IN ACTION

〉

This chip during the CA Championship definitely was from a poor lie. The giveaway? The fact my follow-through is so short. I obviously swung down steeply to penetrate some deep greenside rough, and the turf stopped my clubhead at impact. If my lie were good, you'd for sure see a much fuller finish, with my hands about belt high.

〈

A chip from greenside rough at the 2009 Northern Trust Open. The host course, Riviera Country Club, is noted for it's sticky kikuya grass, which is very difficult to chip from. On this chip, I firmed up my grip and accelerated through impact to make sure my sand wedge didn't get hung up. I was glad to escape with my first win of the year.

〉

This nice up-and-down from a tributary of Rae's Creek got me a birdie on the 13th hole at Augusta National during the 2008 Masters. Chips from tall grass are unusual at Augusta. Notice how I'm getting excellent height for such a short shot. Accelerating through the ball with the clubface kept open will allow you to hit the ball high, even with a short swing.

❮

On this shot, I wanted
the ball to stop quickly
after landing. I hit down
firmly into the back of
the ball, and the sharp
leading edge of the
clubhead then cut like a
knife into the turf. Still,
the bounce along the
sole of my wedge allowed
the clubhead to deflect
off the turf and follow
my hands into the finish.
As always, I made sure
the face of the wedge
remained open well after
the ball was gone.

"One of the secrets to good bunker play
is rhythm. A smooth swing is every bit as
important as your setup and swing mechanics.
If your rhythm is good, your chances of hitting
a good shot increase dramatically."

103

→ SECTION III

Sand Play

ONE OF THE EXTRA BONUSES of playing at the highest level is seeing and hearing the fans react to key shots. The best, of course, is the dead stillness as the last man on the course lines up his putt, followed by the roar that comes as his winning putt drops. That moment of truth, and the reaction to it stays with every player who's been lucky enough to experience it. ›

SOMETIMES A PLAYER WILL hit a big hook from the tee, and we'll see marshals on the right side of the fairway waving and people ducking—only to have the ball end up back in the middle of the fairway. We chuckle, and I'm sure the fans do, too. But often we'll hear a groan after a ball lands in a bunker. That's a natural reaction, too; most amateurs dread being in the sand.

• • •

ONE OF THE BEST BUNKER shots I've ever hit came at the 16th hole in the final round of the Memorial Tournament in 2006. It's a par 3, so when my shot plopped into the sand I groaned right along with the fans. By then it was clear I wasn't going to win the tournament (I finished in a tie for fourth), but the shot was still disappointing, because it was right at the flag, but just short. The ball was buried in the face of the bunker and just under the lip, maybe 15 feet short of the hole. I like this kind of challenge. I drove the wedge into the sand below the ball—the ball popped straight up in the air and released softly right into the cup for a birdie. I couldn't believe it went in. Judging by the fans' reaction, neither could they.

There are times, though, when I deliberately hit into bunkers, particularly on par 5s.

The 15th hole at Augusta is a good example; depending on the wind conditions and pin placement, I'm happy to play for the bunker to the right of the green, because I know I can get up and down from over there. The long 11th hole at the TPC Sawgrass is another good example because that small green can be a tough one to hold. Overall, the sand is a good place to be if the alternative from the fairway is running over the green into big trouble.

Sometimes we can catch a buried lie in the face, as I did at the Memorial, or a downhill lie in the back of the bunker and we're left with an awkward stance. Paul Azinger had a poor lie left of 18 at the 1993 Memorial but famously holed his shot from left of the green and went on to win. Ideally, of course, we're hoping to find a flat spot in a bunker. Bob Tway drew a good lie about 20 yards out on the last hole of the 1986 PGA Championship, lofted a shot onto the green, and it rolled in like a putt to win and crown him Player of the Year.

Those three shots—mine, Paul's, and Bob's—came at varying lengths, but the key for each was the same. When players struggle with bunker shots under pressure down the stretch, they usually leave shots short, because the shots are tentative. The players ease the club into

the ball and don't maintain momentum into the follow-through. The key to success, whether it's from 15 feet or 30 yards, is to make sure you accelerate into the finish and swing aggressively, even if the goal is to have the ball come out and land softly. Especially if you want the ball to land softly.

• • •

IN 2008, I IMPROVED FROM 83rd to third in sand saves. Dave Pelz pointed out that the average bunker shot on tour was 10 yards, so that's what I practiced, building a reference point and a foundation for hitting shots with consistency. Pelz also felt that good bunker play could help driving—we can't have a lot of "hit" in the sand as we do on the tee, so a good rhythm developed in the sand can carry over to other shots. With that improved tempo in the sand, I was able to get more shots closer to the hole and so improve my chances to make the putt, which is the other key element to the sand-save statistic. The first goal is always to get out. But with an understanding of how to play from the bunker, there's no reason not to focus on hitting the shot to within gimme range, and make the crowd go wild.

On long bunker shots, I swing with as much effort as on a full-swing shot.

→ THE 30-FOOT BASE POINT

IN 2008, I GOT UP AND DOWN FROM SAND 80 times in 128 tries. I had one practice-session streak where I hit my bunker shots to within three feet of the hole 28 times in a row. Thanks to Dave Pelz's research showing that the average length of a greenside bunker shot was 30 feet, I began practicing in sand from 30 feet exclusively. By becoming skilled from that distance, it was easy to adapt to shorter and longer shots. By varying a couple of preswing considerations–how open I set the clubface and where I positioned the ball in my stance–I could regulate my distance without changing my technique. Every sand shot is a little different in terms of distance, lie, consistency of the sand, and the height you need to hit the ball, and it's a stimulating area of the game to practice. If you keep the 30-foot baseline distance in mind when you practice, you can't help but improve. In fact, there won't be a lie you can't handle with ease.

CHOOSE THE RIGHT WEDGE

On virtually all sand shots, I prefer a 60-degree sand wedge with a moderate amount of bounce on the sole (the wedge at *far right*). I don't insist you copy me; you may need a little less loft and more bounce. What's important is that you select a sand wedge that inspires confidence and matches the nuances of your swing so you don't fight its basic design characteristics.

IT STARTS WITH GOOD RHYTHM

I've found that when my sand play is good, it carries over into my driving. Although the two swings aren't much alike technically, they both require good rhythm. With bunker play especially, it's crucial that you have a smooth tempo and swing through the ball rather than at it. Rather than use raw force, learn to trust your technique and the design of the club to get the ball out.

→ HINGE & HOLD

MANY AMATEURS BELIEVE the swing from sand is different than the swing they use on standard wedge shots from the fairway. That isn't the case at all. In fact, there are a lot more similarities than differences, especially concerning the hinge-and-hold method. On all shots from sand, you hinge your wrists early in the backswing and limit how far you swing your arms. Only use as much speed as is necessary, which in most cases is less than you might think. On the forward swing, try to maintain the hinge in your wrists, controlling distance by how fast you swing your arms through impact into the follow-through. Above all, it's important that you accelerate through the sand. Never– and I mean never–stop your hands at impact. The idea is to make the club-head increase its speed at a steady rate from start to finish. You'll be surprised at how little effort it takes to extricate your ball from sand and get the ball within the three-foot circle.

A PLAIN-VANILLA ADDRESS POSITION

If you study my setup in photo **(A)** and ignore the fact I'm in the bunker, you'd have a hard time distinguishing this shot from a 20-yard pitch. Everything from ball position, to clubface position, to my slightly open stance is the same.

HINGE WRISTS EARLY

My takeaway is simply a matter of cocking the
wrists while swinging the arms back far enough
to accommodate the length of the shot (B). It's a
relaxed, easy action, with little conscious effort.

A STRAIGHT-LINE FINISH

As on standard chips and pitches, the clubhead never
passes the hands, even into the follow-through (C).
Because I've swung the clubhead down the target line,
my club and arms extend toward the target at the finish.

→ RULE NO. 1: MAINTAIN BOUNCE

IN SAND, THE CLUBFACE MUST BE in the same position at impact that you established at address. In fact, it remains in the same open position well into your follow-through, long after the ball is gone. One reason is to maintain loft. You programmed a certain trajectory by adjusting the clubface at address, and you don't want that loft to be any different when the club enters the sand. An even more important reason is to keep the bounce along the club's sole unchanged. If you rotate the clubface closed through impact, you change how the clubhead behaves when it passes through the sand. Instead of the sole of the club riding through the sand without much resistance, the sharp leading edge is brought into play, and the clubhead digs deeply into the sand behind the ball, or else there is too much bounce. Either way, the shot is ruined. You end up taking too much sand, and the ball either comes up short of the hole or you blade it over the green.

PREPROGRAM CLUBFACE LOFT

The clubface at address should always be open to some degree (*top right*), both to create loft and to elevate the leading edge of the clubface above the surface of the sand. When you play the shot, keep the clubface in the open position by resisting the urge to rotate your hands. Even after the ball is gone and the clubhead has passed my forward foot (*bottom right*), the clubface is still facing the target. This holds true on every bunker shot.

DIFFERENT VIEW, SAME STORY

You can see the rounded mass along the sole of the clubhead (*near right*), located just below the leading edge. When the clubhead penetrates the sand, the sole literally bounces off it so the clubhead continues forward. If the clubface closes, the leading edge is lowered and digs, effectively taking the sole out of play. That's why you try to keep the clubface open through impact (*far right*).

→ RULE NO. 2: ACCELERATE!

IT'S ABSOLUTELY NECESSARY TO KEEP YOUR HANDS moving through impact into the finish. If your hands stop at impact, you will release the club early. Too much of the sole will be exposed at impact, and the clubhead will deflect off the sand and into the ball, leading to a skulled shot that airmails the green. Accelerate your hands through impact and you have a much better chance of preserving the clubface position you programmed at address. The clubhead will penetrate the sand at the correct angle and will move through the sand without too much resistance. Remember, when I say "accelerate," I don't mean swing with a tremendous amount of effort. I simply mean that the pace of your swing should increase steadily throughout the downswing so that the momentum carries your hands into a full, free finish.

EXTEND HANDS AFTER IMPACT

Notice how my hands continue moving straight up the target line after the ball is gone (*right*). My trailing arm has straightened, proof that I've accelerated aggressively through impact. I always have the feeling of hitting through the sand rather than trying to dig the ball out. I'm generating plenty of speed, but I'm doing it with finesse rather than sheer force.

DON'T ROTATE YOUR HANDS

See in the photo at left how the back of my glove is facing the target? This is proof my hands have continued to travel along the path they followed through impact. They don't stop here, either—they keep going until the momentum of the forward swing eases up later in the follow-through. Notice also that my leading arm and the clubshaft form a straight line, indicating the clubhead hasn't passed my hands. Finally, notice the position of the clubface amid the flying sand. It remains open, just as it was at address. If the toe of your sand wedge points toward the sky after impact, chances are the club did some digging earlier. That means trouble.

→ A CUSHION OF SAND

ONE OF THE FIRST THINGS THE BEGINNING GOLFER LEARNS is that sand shots are one of the few shots (the pitch from deep rough is another) where the clubhead doesn't make contact with the ball. The clubhead enters the sand behind the ball and sends it flying toward the target on a cushion of sand. So exactly how far behind the ball should the clubhead make contact, and how steep an angle should the clubhead be traveling along when it enters the sand? Both questions are impossible to answer in a general way because they depend on the firmness and type of sand, the quality of your lie, and the distance you want to hit the shot. But I'll say this: If you accelerate your arms, hands, and the clubhead through impact, a lot of complications are solved automatically. Practice and experience will take care of the rest.

RETRACING AN OPTIMAL SWING PATH

Having played a shot and taken a divot (*sequence below*), I'm retracing the path my clubhead followed through impact. The ball outside the divot references my ball position. Notice how the clubface is open as it enters the sand, and how it remains open until it exits. With the sole of the clubhead exposed and the bounce in play, I don't worry about the club digging too deeply.

LET THE CLUB
DO THE WORK

Some players prefer to hit down fairly sharply into the sand; others like the clubhead traveling at a very shallow angle. Some like to hit as far as six inches behind the ball, others may take only an inch of sand. On a standard bunker shot with a good lie and fairly firm sand (*left*), I like to make contact about three to four inches behind the ball and take a divot that usually "feels" deeper than it turns out to be. I allow the club to behave the way it was designed, with the bounce along the sole of the clubhead preventing it from penetrating so deeply that it kills my acceleration.

→ THE DOWNHILL LIE

UNEVEN LIES IN SAND ARE ESPECIALLY CHALLENGING. The downhill lie is especially troubling to the everyday player. Unlike chips and pitches from turf, mishits can be pretty unforgiving. Bunkers are classified as hazards for a reason, and if you hit the shot excessively fat or thin, the consequences are often more severe than a similar miss from grass. The most common tendency is to hit the ball fat, which in most cases means it doesn't escape the bunker at all. If you overcompensate and blade the shot, you'll either drive the ball into the face of the bunker or else fly the green. The key to handling the downhill lie is to effectively turn it into a level lie by adjusting your body angles and weight distribution, and maintaining them throughout the swing.

LEAN TOWARD THE TARGET AT ADDRESS

Start by setting your upper body perpendicular to the downhill slope, leaning toward the target so virtually all of your weight is on your forward foot (*right*). Position the ball forward in your stance, because that will encourage you to swing on a steep, downward angle, parallel to the slope. Remember to open the clubface.

TRY TO PASS THE ONE-FOOT TEST AT ADDRESS

At address your weight should be distributed so emphatically onto your forward foot that you can lift your rear foot off the ground without losing your balance (*left*). This one-foot test sets the stage not just for address, but for the swing itself. Throughout a two-foot swing, the majority of your weight will remain on your forward foot. You do not shift your weight onto your rear foot at all. In fact, your rear foot is only on the ground to assist you in keeping your balance.

SET THE STAGE FOR A STEEP APPROACH

Because I've positioned the ball well forward in my stance (*below*), the only way to reach it on the downswing is to keep my weight on my front foot and come into the ball on a steep angle. By moving my swing center forward, I now can avoid hitting the ball fat.

THE DOWNHILL LIE

→ KEEP
WEIGHT
FORWARD

THE BACKSWING IS THE SAME as for a normal pitch. This shot does not require a great deal of force. Use the hinge-and-hold method, cocking your wrists and limiting your arm swing. At all times the lion's share of your weight remains on your forward foot. There is no weight shift onto your rear foot, in part because you don't need the raw power, but also because the momentum would cause you to lose your balance. It's important that you keep the angle of your spine perpendicular to the sand, as opposed to tilting it slightly away from the target as if the lie were level.

LIMIT ACTION IN HIPS, LEGS

On any uneven lie, it's important to keep your lower body stable. In the photo (*left*), notice how my hips haven't turned very much and my front foot remains planted firmly, just as it was at address. By keeping your lower body quiet and your weight forward, you're better able to maintain your balance, which in turn makes it easier to control the club on the downswing. Another feature is how vertical the clubshaft is. As I hinge my wrists, the club is cocked upward. This is a sign that I'll swing the club down on a pretty steep angle.

THE DOWNHILL LIE

→ SWING STEEP, STAY DOWN

ON DOWNHILL LIES, YOU WANT THE CLUB to travel steeply downward through impact. I find that if I am leaning toward the target at address, it makes it easier to hit down sharply and avoid taking too much sand, or not enough. Leaning toward the target also regulates how deeply the clubhead penetrates the sand and ensures that the lowest point of my arc isn't too far behind the ball or too far in front of it. From a downhill lie, you want to be able to make a nice, long divot as opposed to a short, deep one. Adjusting your setup as I explained isn't quite enough, however. Leaning toward the target helps you deal with the slope but doesn't overcome it entirely. You need to make a conscious effort to keep the clubhead low after impact. You want to stay with the shot and resist the tendency to let the club come up too abruptly after the ball has left the target and is tracking toward the flagstick.

TWO KEYS TO GETTING HEIGHT

Downhill lies usually occur near the back of the bunker, which means you have to carry the ball farther than normal to reach the green. The first key is to accelerate your hands (A), which helps you generate enough clubhead speed to propel the ball forward. Second, make sure you establish plenty of clubface loft by opening the face at address, and preserving that loft well after the ball is gone (B).

HOW LOW CAN YOU GO?

When you swing steeply down into the ball, concentrate on keeping your head and upper body down through impact. It takes effort to stay down as your hands extend into the follow-through. I try to keep my head down until my hands are at waist height on my follow-through (*left*). After impact, go ahead and release your lower body by allowing the heel of your rear foot to come off the ground. Eventually the momentum of the swing will carry you into the finish (*inset*). You may find you push the ball a bit to the side of the target. If so, adjust your aim at address.

→ MASTERING THE TRICKY UPHILL LIE

PLAYING THE UPHILL LIE is similar to the downhill lie in that you need to accommodate your body to fit the slope. Amateurs typically hit the uphill lie fat, hitting behind the ball and taking too much sand. The result is that they fail to get the quick elevation they need to clear the lip of the bunker and make the ball settle within three feet of the flagstick. Like the downhill lie, the shot is performed almost exclusively with the upper body, the legs remaining quiet. If you perform it properly, you should have no trouble achieving the quick height you need to escape the sand. In addition to establishing plenty of loft by opening the clubface at address, you are also tilting your upper body toward your back foot, which effectively adds even more loft to the clubface. With that, it's a shot that requires practice to instill confidence.

THE SECRET IS
IN THE SETUP

The setup is just the opposite of the downhill lie. You set your upper body perpendicular to the sideslope (*left*), this time placing most of your weight on your rear foot (*opposite*). The purpose is to program a swing in which the clubhead travels on a shallow, almost level angle through the sand. As there is a lot of stress on your rear foot, make sure it is placed securely into the sand. I don't play the ball as far forward as with the downhill lie, because the center of my swing is more toward the center of my stance. I set my feet only slightly open, to make it easier to swing the club straight up the target line on the downswing.

THE UPHILL LIE

→ BALANCE IS CRITICAL

THE FLOW OF MY BACKSWING naturally puts some stress on my rear foot, which is flared outward a bit to accept the force. I make no effort to stay centered directly above the ball, and I allow my upper body to drift a bit toward my rear foot.

The swing itself must be smooth, slow, and rhythmic, allowing everything to fall together deliberately. This is crucial in helping keep my balance and deliver the club into the sand with speed and accuracy. I use the hinge-and-hold method, cocking my wrists generously while, this time, allowing my arms to swing back a bit farther than normal to help me generate a bit more speed on the forward swing. Good balance is crucial.

KEEP SPEED CONTROLLED

Because the clubface has an exceptional amount of loft, you need to generate lots of speed (*above*) to help the ball fly forward as well as up. Thus, I'm taking a shallow divot so there's as little resistance from the sand as possible. I'm also applying some effort with my legs and hips; compare the difference between my front leg in the photo above with the active role they are taking in the photo at right. Although I'm faithful to the hinge-and-hold method, I'm applying a great deal of speed with my arms, making sure the clubhead trails my hands all the way. The speed transfers to my hands and clubhead, sending the sand and ball flying.

THE UPHILL LIE

→ # FINISH SHOWS CONTROL

THE FINISH OF THE UPHILL SHOT will test your ability to overcome gravity, since you must shift your weight partially onto your forward foot–no small feat considering you're moving everything uphill. Note how my divot is very uniform (*right*), with consistent depth from beginning to end. This resulted from setting my body perpendicular to the sand at address. Very often, the amateur tends to drive the clubhead head-on into the sand, the leading edge digging deeply. It rarely works. The sand brings the clubhead to a dead stop and the ball stays in the bunker. Another tendency is not allowing for a slightly pulled shot. That happens naturally, so adjust your aim at address.

A FULL, EXTENDED FOLLOW-THROUGH

Although my hands aren't particularly high at this stage of the follow-through (*right*), they clearly are extended, a sign that I've accelerated my arms and hands aggressively. My balance helped me make nice contact with the sand.

RESULT: A HIGH, SOFT FLOATER

Watching the ball float high and soft toward the flagstick is especially satisfying when you do it from a sloping lie. There are three things worth noting in the photo at near left. First is the completeness of my follow-through. Because my swing had plenty of freedom, I generated plenty of speed and was able to attain a high ball flight and full finish. Second, notice that the heel of my rear foot has come off the ground, proof of a full release of my lower body. This was no chip shot, folks. It required almost a full swing with no loss of precision. Finally, the ball came out a little to the left of the flagstick. That's because I allowed for a slight pull, and I happened to hit this shot dead straight!

→ UPHILL & PLUGGED

BURIED LIES CHANGE the nature of the shot completely. It's impossible to have as much control over the shot as when the ball is sitting up, because you can't apply backspin. Thus, you can't determine precisely how far the ball will roll when it hits the green. With time and practice the shot becomes more predictable, but hitting a high percentage of these shots within three feet of the hole is difficult, if not impossible.

The technique for playing the uphill, buried lie differs from the nice uphill lie in three ways. First, I don't want a shallow angle of approach, because the club won't penetrate the sand deeply enough to get under the ball. Second— and it's related to the first point—I want to distribute my weight onto my front foot, so I can drive the clubhead directly into the bank. Finally, I want my hands to lead the way into impact. That means my finish will be very abrupt, due to the sand bringing the club to a quick stop after impact.

PROGRAM A MORE LEVEL ANGLE OF ATTACK

Although in the photo I'm leaning my upper body slightly away from the target, the majority of my weight is on my front foot. My clubface is open, not to bring the bounce into play, but to create loft. Getting the ball in the air is a challenge, and you will need all the help you can get!

MAKE A SHORT, FORCEFUL SWING

You don't want a long backswing here, because precise contact is important. But you do want to generate some power. Here, I'm turning my hips a little and rotating my shoulders more than usual (A). I swing down firmly and aggressively, aiming about two inches behind the ball (B).

A STRAIGHT-LINE FINISH

As on standard chips and pitches, the clubhead never passes the hands, even into the follow-through. Because I've swung the clubhead down the target line, my club and arms extend toward the target at the finish (C).

THE UPHILL LIE

→ DRIVE CLUBHEAD INTO BANK

THIS IS NO TIME TO BE SHY. There is some finesse here in terms of making the club enter the sand exactly where you're aiming, but mostly it's a case of applying speed and strength. The important thing is that your hands lead the clubhead, which as you can see trails behind. The purpose of leading with the hands is to keep the sharp leading edge of the clubhead exposed, so it can knife into the sand. If I released the club early so my left arm and the clubshaft formed a straight line, the sole of the club would enter the sand first. The sole is too blunt and rounded to penetrate the sand deeply enough to pass under the ball. Your objective is to drive the clubhead directly into the bank on almost a horizontal angle, rather than following the slope as you did when the ball was sitting up.

CLUBHEAD DOESN'T PASS HANDS

The uphill shot with the ball buried is an unusual shot, but I still utilize the hinge-and-hold technique. Always preserve the angle between your lead arm and the clubshaft.

A TALE OF TWO FINISHES

The contrast in finishes between the nice uphill lie and the buried uphill lie is dramatic. With the buried lie (A), my hands were brought to a sudden halt due to driving the clubhead into the uphill slope. That isn't the case when the ball is sitting up (B); with less resistance from the sand, I'm able to follow through with my arms and hands extending into a full, uninhibited finish.

→ THE LONG BUNKER SHOT

MOST AMATEURS BELIEVE the 20- to 50-yard bunker shot is the toughest shot in golf. I've never thought it was particularly difficult, though obviously the sheer distance of the shot does make getting the ball inside the three-foot circle more challenging than on a routine greenside bunker shot. Why does the long bunker shot give so many amateurs (and some pros) fits? From what I've seen, most of them feel they need to alter their technique to achieve the extra distance. The most common mistake results from a fear of taking too much sand and leaving the shot short. So many amateurs try to pick the ball cleanly off the sand, which leads to a lot of skulled shots. Another mistake is moving the ball back in their stance, which beginners do in order to deloft the club and hit the ball farther. I see other errors, and in fact there are a lot of ways to play the long bunker shot poorly. But as you'll see, there is only one way to play the long sand shot well.

TIME TO LET IT FLY

The long bunker shot is the one play in sand where you pull out all the stops. It's very much like playing a full-swing shot from the fairway, with full body rotation, hefty arm swing, and a full hinging of the wrists. The speed and complete freedom of the swing is reflected in your follow-through; it should show full extension (*right*) with your hands continuing into a high, balanced finish.

SETUP SIMILAR TO OTHER SHOTS

The first key to the long bunker shot is to approach it like a routine bunker shot. Play the ball forward in your stance and open the face of your sand wedge (*left, top*), though perhaps a bit less than for a short greenside shot. The other dimensions of your setup are ordinary, but because you're going to be making a longer swing to hit the ball farther, your footing has to be very secure. Make sure your feet are settled into the sand well enough to give you a firm base.

IMPORTANCE OF BALL POSITION

Always position the ball forward on the long bunker shot (*left, bottom*). As on other shots, you're going to deliberately hit a few inches behind the ball. The club will not dig deeply, however, and you'll have no problem getting the ball airborne on a thin cushion of sand. The speed of the swing will minimize resistance from the sand through impact.

CALL IT COURAGE

BECAUSE YOU NEED TO CARRY the ball a healthy distance, it follows that you need to make a longer backswing in order to generate sufficient clubhead speed. The longer swing can be unnerving to the average player, because it induces the feeling you're losing precision and the ability to swing the club through the ball just right. In truth, the margin for error is pretty generous. So long as your setup is sound, your swing rhythm is good, and you accelerate through the ball, you can actually hit the shot a shade thin or heavy and get a decent result. The best way to become comfortable making long swings in sand is to practice, using the keys I outline here.

KEYS TO HELP CONSISTENCY

I prefer to use a 60-degree sand wedge for the long bunker shot, but I'm not limited to that club exclusively. When I sense I can't carry the ball far enough, I don't alter my setup, swing, or ball position in any way. Instead, I simply take more club—my 55-degree sand wedge, for instance, or even a pitching wedge if the shot is near the 50-yard limit. If it's any longer, only then will I consider taking less sand.

A

Think the shot through. Always assess your lie and the quality of the sand before you prepare to hit the shot.

B

Accelerate your arms and hands. Slowing them at any time is the kiss of death.

C

Maintain the clubface position through impact. If you rotate the clubface closed, the leading edge will dig into the sand, ruining the shot.

→ A FANTASTIC FINISH

YOUR FOLLOW-THROUGH REVEALS WHAT HAPPENED earlier in your swing. Very often, you can tell what type of shot a golfer has played simply by looking at his positions just after impact, into the follow-through and at the finish. Examining video of my swing, I can tell whether I was playing a draw or fade, or hitting it high or low, by examining the position of the club and my body after the ball is gone. When I check my follow-through on the long bunker shot, I want to see proof that I swung aggressively, with plenty of acceleration. I look for four signs: (1) that both of my arms are straight by the time my hands reach waist height; (2) my belt buckle is facing the target; (3) my hands finish above my head; and (4) the heel of my back foot has come off the ground. All of these are signs of good rhythm and a well-coordinated downswing–real musts when playing the long bunker shot.

STRIVE FOR EXTENSION, HIGH HANDS

Full extension of your arms (*below*) is a sign you hit through the ball rather than at it. It also indicates you swung with enough speed to carry the ball 20 yards or more. From there, the hands continue into a relaxed, high finish. If your finish doesn't look like mine, you probably stopped everything at impact, which means leaving the ball short or failing to get out of the sand altogether.

FINISH SHOWS TOTAL FREEDOM

Here's the look you
want. It shows total
freedom and relaxation.
It indicates I had no
tension at any time
earlier in my swing, and I
didn't inhibit any part of
my body from responding
to the speed and effort
I applied earlier.

Technically, there are
a few features worth
noting. Notice my front
foot is still in the same
position it was in at
address, with no twisting
that would displace the
sand. The heel of my
rear foot has risen in
response to my weight
shift and high finish.
My hips have unwound
completely, and my
shoulders have rotated
even more. Finally, look
at my hands. I'm not
holding the club too
tightly, and the back
of my gloved hand still
faces away from me—a
clue that I didn't rotate
the club to a closed
position, even on the
follow-through.

→ THE BURIED LIE

NO SHOT IN SAND GIVES AMATEURS FITS like the buried lie. Most amateur golfers get discouraged just looking at one, and their confidence shrinks even more when they prepare to get the ball out. But the buried lie isn't as tough as it looks. Sure, it's harder to get the ball close to the hole because it comes out like a knuckleball, with no spin at all. Thus, it's difficult to tell exactly how far the ball will roll. But as far as getting the ball out of the bunker, a couple of keys will ensure that you escape every time. What's more, you should be able to achieve some nice height on the shot, which most amateurs find impossible, not because of the lie, but because of faulty technique. The most common error is to try to help the ball into the air by swinging up on it. If you're having trouble, you may be trying to muscle the ball out and swing harder than is necessary, which leads to poor contact. The key to success is good technique, not brute force.

ADDRESS IS CRUCIAL

Position the ball forward of center in your stance (*above left*), and open the face of your sand wedge at address. It's important that you position your hands forward so the shaft leans toward the target. That exposes the sharp leading edge, which will knife into the sand (*above right*). At the same time, the open clubface will help you create enough loft to get the ball into the air.

THE MOMENT OF TRUTH

Position the slight majority of your weight on your front foot and keep it there throughout the swing. Use the hinge-and-hold technique and deliver a firm downward blow, the hands ahead of the clubhead at impact (*left*). So long as your hands lead the way, the clubhead will penetrate the sand to a point below the level of the ball (*above*) and make the ball come out along with a layer of sand. You should be able to identify the logo on the ball; that's proof the ball comes out with no spin. You should feel like the clubhead continues to move downward even after the ball pops into the air.

The buried lie is the one sand shot where you want the clubhead to penetrate deeply into the sand. It doesn't dig so deeply that the sand brings the clubhead to a stop, but it should descend to a point lower than the bottom of the ball.

→ LOW FINISH A SIGN OF SUCCESS

BURIED LIES USUALLY OCCUR in fluffy, coarse sand that often is a little moist. It can be on the heavy side, which can make it even more difficult to penetrate if you don't hit down on the sand with the leading edge in play. Remember my thought on how the follow-through reflects what occurred earlier in the swing? It's very much the case with the buried lie. If your follow-through is nice and low, with your hands never coming up higher than your waist (*right*), this offers proof positive that your clubhead traveled on a downward arc through the sand and beyond. Think of the low finish when you practice.

EXPECT A LOW, RUNNING SHOT

It's healthy to have high expectations, but at the same time you must be realistic. From the buried lie, the ball won't stop quickly when it lands. It will always fly lower (*left*) than when playing from a nice, clean lie. The final key to making the most of the buried lie is to form a sound strategy. If there's a high lip directly in front of you, play away from it, even if it means not aiming directly at the hole. If you're playing to a tight hole location with little green to work with, don't get cute. The three-foot circle that is always our goal can be elusive at times, and there are occasions when we have to take our medicine.

LESSONS
IN ACTION

I'm playing a high, soft bunker shot from a good lie. Note that my facial expression isn't strained and that my arms and hands are relaxed. The length of my follow-through shows I accelerated through the ball, but I didn't swing all out. The sand is flying, proof that I hit a few inches behind the ball. Never try to pick the ball clean on a short shot.

This long bunker shot was at the outside limit of the 50-yard range. I've swung with all of the speed I possess and every part of my body has gotten into the act. I've achieved a very thin, shallow divot. If I'd taken any more sand, the ball would have come up woefully short, any less and I'd surely have airmailed the green.

Another long bunker shot. If you removed the sand from this photograph, it would be easy to mistake this for a shot from the fairway. Note that I'm not using my 60-degree wedge here; the sheer length of the shot has demanded that I use a club with less loft. My footing on a shot of this length has to be rock solid; I really twist my feet into the sand.

Another greenside
bunker explosion:
This shot required a
combination of both
height and distance.
Again, I've accelerated
my arms and hands
decisively, and the
manner in which they're
coming up in my follow-
through shows that
I concentrated hard on
keeping the clubface
open through impact.
In fact, the clubface is
still open relative to
my arms and hands!

"In pitching, you control the distance of
the shot by how far open you adjust the clubface
at address, your ball position, and how fast
you swing your arms."

149

→ SECTION IV

Pitching

I HAD A FEELING I WAS GOING to enjoy the final round of the 2006 Masters because I was playing well. I also had a one-stroke lead and the perfect fellow competitor, my old friend Fred Couples. But no matter how I felt on the first tee, I knew I was going to have to hit a lot of good shots. As much as I enjoy Fred's company, he was only one shot back and there were seven others within two. I was going to enjoy the walk, but by no means did I think it was going to be a walk in the park. ›

WE WERE TIED AFTER FREDDIE birdied the first hole, and we both parred around to the seventh. I hit a wedge to about eight feet, Freddie hit his to about four, and we both birdied to remain tied. I love the opportunities to score on the back nine, but I was starting to feel in need of a boost. Freddie was playing very well and two-time Masters champ Jose Maria Olazabal was only one behind.

My second shot on the par 5 eighth hole came up short of the green, a good 40 yards from the pin. That was in the back portion of the green, which has a ridge across the middle of it. Fred reached the green in two but was short of the ridge and had a long, difficult putt for eagle. The challenge for me was to carry the ridge but stop the ball from running over the back.

• • •

I'D SEEN A SHOT A LOT LIKE this a few years earlier at Augusta, on No. 11. That day I was chasing the leaders and had no room for error. My approach landed to the right and past the green, a little left of where Larry Mize made his chip to win the playoff against Greg Norman

in 1987. Larry's great, running chip was played off a mound, which killed the speed, and the ball rolled into the hole for birdie. My shot, though, was going to have to carry a portion of the back bunker with spin to slow it on its way downhill to the front left of the hole—and the water just beyond that.

In both cases, as in most at Augusta, the lies were pretty tight, which meant that the ball had to be clipped perfectly to have control over the length of the shot and to impart enough spin to apply the brakes once the ball started rolling downhill. But it also had to have enough height and distance to carry the trouble in front of me.

• • •

WEDGE SHOTS OF 30 TO 50 yards, sometimes called half-wedges, can cause trouble for a lot of players. The tendency seems to be either to take almost a full wedge backswing and decelerate on the downswing, or else get too handsy and allow the clubhead to pass the hands on the downswing. That's the very last thing we want to happen on these shots.

They're actually just hinge-and-hold chips with elongated swings. Not a full swing, just longer than a chip. Like a chip, once we break our wrists and accelerate our hands into the

finish, the arm and club are traveling the same speed, making distance control easy. And when the leading edge and the bounce of the club are consistent for a longer period of time through impact, these shots come off much more consistently. This all allows us, with plenty of practice, to know how far the ball is going to fly on shots of anywhere from 30 to 50 yards. And when we know that, we can focus on getting the shot inside the three-foot circle, where we know we can make putts.

My pitch on No. 11 carried about 25 yards over the mound and bunker. Its spin deadened its momentum and the ball rolled in for a surprise birdie to keep me close to the leaders that day. I didn't catch them; I finished third.

The shot on No. 8 in 2006 didn't go in, but it did carry nearly the entire 40 yards and stopped on a dime a foot from the cup. When Freddie three-putted for par and I tapped in for a birdie, I had the lead, renewed confidence, and about two hours later my second green jacket.

Longer chips require a more aggressive swing, and a longer follow-through.

→ BACK TO BASICS

THE PITCH SHOT IS LITTLE MORE THAN an elongated chip. The fundamentals are exactly the same as the chip, and the swing technique is based on the same philosophy. So how is a pitch different than the basic chip we covered earlier? The difference is the length and speed of the swing, which ultimately make it possible to produce a wider variety of shots than is possible with the chipping motion. The pitching swing is longer in terms of your arm swing, wrist cock, shoulder turn, and footwork. As a result, you generate much more clubhead speed. When you add speed to the equation, a new world opens up in terms of what you can do with the ball. With speed comes the possibility of increasing your backspin, hitting the ball higher than normal, and producing good shots from difficult lies. The pitch includes high, soft shots from around the greens and the half-wedge from 30 to 50 yards–a shot that gives most amateurs fits.

WRIST HINGE PLAYS KEY ROLL ON ALL PITCHES

Breaking your wrists is mandatory on all short game shots, but the action plays an even more crucial role as the length of your swing increases (*below, right*). Although you never consciously uncock your wrists, they do release to some degree through impact. The more clubhead speed required, the more you hinge your wrists–and the more speed you apply as the clubhead passes through the ball at impact.

SHOT LENGTH DICTATES SETUP

Even before I begin the backswing, you can tell the type of shot I'm playing by examining two parts of my setup. One is my ball position; when it's farther back, near the middle of my stance (*near right*), it's clear I'm playing a low-flying shot. Second is my clubface position. The fact I've aligned the leading edge fairly square to the target is another clue that I'm planning on bringing the ball in on a lower, more commanding trajectory.

SHAFT LEANS FORWARD THROUGH IMPACT

Because pitch shots can stretch up to 50 yards, it's easy to give in to the tendency of applying extra speed with your hands. You can't get away with that; your hands must be ahead of the ball at impact. A sure sign of that: The shaft of the club leans toward the target when the clubhead meets the ball. If the shaft is leaning backward away from the target, it's a sure sign of poor contact.

"TRAPPING" LEADS TO GREAT BALL FLIGHT

One of the main purposes of leading with your hands and having the shaft lean toward the target is the crisp kind of impact it promotes. You want to "trap" the ball against the clubface, compressing the ball efficiently so it rebounds with plenty of backspin and a straight ball trajectory. If you strike the ball solidly, you have better distance control, especially when the wind is blowing.

→ FUNDAMENTALS NEVER CHANGE

AT FIRST GLANCE, THE BEST PLAYERS IN THE WORLD give the impression of having swing styles that are vastly different. For sure, there's no mistaking the swings of Vijay Singh and Padraig Harrington. But with their short games especially, appearances can be deceiving. Although Vijay and Padraig (and I, for that matter) vary a lot in terms of rhythm, tempo, and our mannerisms, we're very much the same from a technical standpoint. If you view slow-motion videos of all three of us, you'll notice that on pitch shots the length of our backswings is shorter than our follow-throughs, especially on shorter shots. Our hands are always ahead of the clubhead at impact, and all of us maintain some degree of hinge on our wrists well after the ball is gone. If you want to learn something from watching top players on TV, you need to train your eyes to spot the right things. The fundamentals are what matter. The rest is just window dressing.

MAINTAIN ANGLE ON SHORT PITCHES

On full-swing shots with the driver and fairway woods, players often exert power with every part of their body, their hands included. In that case, you sometimes will see the clubhead passing the hands on the follow-through. But on pitch shots, the clubhead always lags behind (*right*). The reason is control. You're trying to hit the ball a specific distance, and you can do that well only if you keep your hands quiet.

THE LONGER THE SHOT, THE GREATER THE EXTENSION

The increased swing speed of the longer pitches should be reflected by your arms extending fully on the follow-through (*above*). Both arms should straighten, with the club staying in line with both of them. This is possible only if your hands keep moving through impact. Never stop your hands abruptly (*left*). It ruins your chances of hitting a good shot right there.

SQUARE UP CLUBFACE FOR LONGER, LOWER PITCHES

A sound way to regulate distance and vary your trajectory is to adjust the position of your clubface at address (*below*). By setting the clubface square, I can decrease loft even more by moving the ball back in my stance or moving my hands farther forward at address.

→ SECRETS OF DISTANCE CONTROL

SOMETIMES YOU CONTROL DISTANCE by lengthening or shortening your swing. I do that myself on occasion, but I've found my touch has to be especially good to pull it off. A more effective technique–especially in the tricky 30- to 50-yard range–is to alter your ball position and adjust the position of the clubface at address. By making adjustments in those two areas, you can vary your distances tremendously without

When I want a higher trajectory, I open the clubface and move the ball farther forward in my stance (*below*). After making these adjustments, I make my normal swing. Never try to hit the ball high by changing your swing—especially hitting up on the ball through impact.

changing the length or speed of your swing. It takes practice and experimentation, and there are rules. I don't like "shutting down" the clubface by closing it beyond square; it's better to switch to a club with less loft. Nor do I like to position the ball to the rear of center in my stance, since I can make solid contact only with an excessively steep swing. Mix up your ball and clubface positions. It's fun and very productive.

There are two flagsticks on the green I'm playing to in the images at right. On this shot, I'm aiming for the flagstick at left, which is located just atop a tier on the back portion of the green. Trying to fly the ball all the way to that flagstick and stop it quickly would be very difficult. If it comes up short, it won't roll to the front of the green, and flying it too far means a dangerous downhill putt. The better choice is to bring the ball in low, landing it in the middle of the green and letting it run up the tier and close to the hole. I've programmed the low shot by squaring up the clubface and playing the ball in the center of my stance. It isn't necessary to play the ball farther back than that.

→ MIX UP YOUR SHOT SELECTION

THE TYPE OF SHOT YOU PLAY INTO THE GREEN depends on many factors. There's a tendency among amateurs to put too much emphasis on the raw yardage from the fairway to the middle of the green, which actually can work against you. The hole location, the direction and speed of the wind, the firmness of the green, the design of the green itself (many are two-tiered), and the general slope of the putting surface all

MAKE A SHORT, CRISP BACKSWING

Because I'm hitting the ball low and driving the ball forward with a delofted clubface, I don't need as much clubhead speed as on a shot with a higher trajectory. So, using the customary hinge-and-hold technique, I keep my backswing short and crisp. I cock my wrists early in the takeaway and let them hinge fully, but I limit how far back I swing my arms. Note the appearance of the clubhead here. The leading edge is aiming more toward the ground than the sky, proof that the clubface is square rather than fanned wide open. On this type of pitch, you want to keep your lower body quiet and avoid making much of a shoulder turn.

should be taken into account. They will determine how far you want to carry the ball, the type of trajectory you seek, and how much spin you apply. Over the next several pages, I'll show how I play two different types of shots from the same spot in the fairway. I'm playing to a green that is 40 yards deep, and the hole locations are radically different. Each demands a different type of flight to get the ball within the three-foot circle.

On a low-flying shot, you really want to trap the ball against the clubface to accentuate solid contact. With the ball played in the center of your stance, your downswing will be fairly steep, and you should hit down firmly into the back of the ball. You can tell by the explosive appearance of my divot at right how I accelerated into the ball, and sent it sizzling on a low trajectory toward that back pin. I have kept the clubface in the same square position I established at address, and have led the swing with my arms and hands.

HIGH PITCH

→ DRIVE DOWN & THROUGH

ALTHOUGH MANY PLAYERS REFER TO THIS SHOT as a "punch," I don't think of it that way. To me, a punch shot is one where you terminate the swing at impact and deliberately cut off your follow-through. I dislike that style, because it implies a very handsy technique in which you're throwing the clubhead into the ball. At best, it results in a poor shaft angle at impact and adds loft to the clubface. At worst, you decelerate and the

On a low pitch, I direct the force of the swing downward sharply through impact (*left*). That, combined with the fact I'm not swinging with a tremendous amount of effort, results in a low, short follow-through, my hands just above waist height. Although the ball came off the clubface with plenty of speed, it has a lot of backspin, too. It will come into the green fast, take two bounces, and then check up a bit on the third bounce. The ball will have just enough momentum to climb the tier and settle next to the hole, within the three-foot circle that is always the goal on challenging pitch shots like this one.

clubhead passes your hands—a recipe for disaster. Remember, you are hitting down and through the ball, not at it. As on all shots, it is absolutely criticial that you accelerate your hands into the finish. The finish may be short, but your arms, hands, and the clubhead still were gaining speed from the moment they started down. It is the small size of the swing, not a punching action, that leads to the abbreviated follow-through.

→ SECOND HOLE LOCATION: MORE HEIGHT REQUIRED

THE GREEN I'M PLAYING TO IS REALLY TWO GREENS IN ONE. Like many large green complexes, there is a front half and a back half. Both flagsticks are on the back half of the green, but the flagstick on the right–the one I'm firing at now– is about 35 feet farther back than the one on the left. Unlike the flag I played to earlier, I can fly the ball safely onto the back tier, since I have plenty of green to work with and don't need to fear coming up short and having the ball roll back to the front of the green. I could play a low shot to the flagstick on the right, but it doesn't give me as good an opportunity to get the ball within the three-foot circle. The ball flight that fits this challenge is the standard pitch that flies nice and high, thanks to the ample loft of my 60-degree sand wedge.

LONGER CARRY: BALL FORWARD IN STANCE

Although I want a high shot trajectory, I'm not going to extremes–this is not a flop shot. I'm merely playing a normal pitch that takes full advantage of the loft on my 60-degree wedge. I'm playing the ball farther forward in my stance than on the low-flying shot, the ball opposite the instep of my front foot. That one preswing adustment guarantees more clubface loft at impact.

MORE LOFT REQUIRES ADDED SWING SPEED

The higher ball flight I've programmed at address means the ball will expend a lot of its energy traveling upward. But because I need to make the ball fly forward as well, this shot requires more clubhead speed. I do that by lengthening my backswing slightly and then accelerating more aggressively on the downswing than I did on the lower shot. Although the photo may suggest a style with a longer club, I do not *feel* like I'm making the same type of swing I would with, say, a 6-iron. My pitching swing feels like a longer version of a normal chip shot.

When the ball is forward in your stance, you can feel like you have to strain in order to make your swing bottom out at a point beyond the heel of your forward foot. The secret is to lean a little toward your front foot on the downswing (*right*), which moves the center of your swing more forward, toward the ball. You then hit down at a steep angle, all the while moving your hands and the clubhead toward the target. Your hands must be slightly ahead of the ball at impact, so you can trap the ball with the clubhead and really catch it flush. Remember to accelerate steadily; there is no need to rush the downswing.

LOW PITCH

→ KEYS TO A MUST-HAVE SHOT

PITCHING THE BALL TO A HOLE CUT ON A SHELF is one of those shots that looks easy but is difficult for the average player to pull off. Precise distance control is an absolute necessity. You need to apply a lot of backspin, which is always a challenge when you're making less than a full swing. Solid contact is a must but can be elusive due to the tight lies we experience on the firm, well-manicured fairways we see today. The challenge

HIGH FINISH MEANS HIGH TRAJECTORY

Because the swing on the high pitch is fractionally longer than on a short pitch, it follows that your follow-through should be longer, too. At left, my hands are very high at the finish for two reasons. First, I accelerated faster than I did on the shorter, low-flying pitch and the momentum simply created a longer follow-through. Second, because the ball was forward in my stance, my hands came up more abruptly after impact. The two main factors that go into this shot—ball forward in my stance and the steep angle of approach—apply a ton of backspin. The ball will stop quickly after landing.

is pretty stiff, and under pressure most amateurs respond by playing the low shot, which is more forgiving and easier to pull off but less likely to get the ball close. The biggest obstacle is a clear idea of how you want the club to behave on the down-swing. The goal is to attack the ball on a steep angle, despite the ball being forward in your stance. With the right mental picture, the shot becomes much easier to execute.

The look of the out-to-in swing is distinctive, and I'm sure you've seen it before. The player takes the club back to the outside, positioning the clubshaft so it is vertical at the top of the backswing (*right*). Even before you begin the backswing, the chances of a good shot are ruined, because the downswing will be way too steep, with the club approaching the ball along an out-to-in path. The chances of solid contact are cut in half, and even if you do hit the ball solidly, you won't apply efficient backspin. Your direction control will suffer, too.

→ NEVER SWING OUT-TO-IN

ONE TECHNIQUE TAUGHT IN SAND PLAY is having the player open his stance and then swing the club down on an out-to-in path parallel with the feet. As I stated earlier, I dislike that technique and feel the clubhead should travel more toward the target on all short-game shots. To be precise, my clubhead actually travels on a line between my foot alignment and the flagstick. But for your game, you should try to swing the club

OUT-TO-IN SWING PATH: SHANKS A LOT!

When you attack the ball on an out-to-in path with an open clubface, the clubhead arrives at the ball with the hosel leading the way instead of the clubface. You can see the result in the inset and photos at left: the dreaded shank, with the ball squirting off at an oblique angle into even worse trouble. That's the worst-case scenario, but there are other bad outcomes. You're also likely to hit the ball either fat or thin, or else pull it well off line. If you get lucky and hit the ball perfectly, your chances of hitting the distance you hoped aren't very good, and the ball will take a crooked bounce when it lands.

toward the target at the outset, and then refine your swing path as your skills become more developed. But at all costs, get rid of the out-to-in, cut-across-the-ball method I'm showing here. I feel I should give it special attention because it's so common and there's a good chance you'll recognize this technique as your own. It leads to fat and thin shots at best, and a horrifying shank at worst.

THE SHORT, SOFT PITCH

NOW THAT YOU KNOW what not to do on a short pitch requiring a bit of carry and a soft landing, let's focus on the right way to play this shot. The payoffs of doing it correctly are enormous. First, solid contact is a cinch, the clubface catching the ball solidly and imparting true end-over-end backspin that will make the ball land softly and roll directly at the hole. Second, your margin for error is increased because the correct swing is shorter and more compact, with fewer moving parts. That helps your rhythm and timing, and removes a lot of stress. Finally, your touch and feel for distance are excellent, because the club is in a nice, balanced position where you can accelerate it into the ball with just the right amount of speed. One of the truisms in golf is that the correct methods not only produce a better result, they are much easier to execute. That certainly is the case on this shot.

HINGE WRISTS EARLY, SWING BACK INSIDE

Address the ball with a slightly open stance, the clubface aimed squarely at the target **(A)**. Hinge your wrists very early in the takeaway, taking the club back slightly to the inside. Limit your arm swing; you don't need a lot of speed.

(B)

(C)

LEAD WITH HANDS, KEEP CLUBFACE SQUARE

Use the hinge-and-hold technique, making sure you direct your hands and the clubhead directly at the target (B). Note my divot—the particles are flying toward the target, not away from it. The hands lead the way through impact.

ACCELERATION RESULTS IN FULL EXTENSION

To ensure that the ball clears the bunker and checks up quickly after landing, the clubface must be kept square through impact and into the follow-through (C). The acceleration causes both arms to straighten at the finish.

The operative word on the half-wedge shot is "aggressive." Although you aren't hitting the ball a great distance, the last thing you want is a lazy, indifferent backswing followed by a downswing in which you ease the club into the ball. Start using the four-step procedure I outlined earlier in this section. How much you open the clubface depends on the length of the shot. Then make a short backswing with a full hinging of your wrists.

→ THE HATED HALF-WEDGE

ONE OF THE MOST FEARED SHOTS IN GOLF is the 30- to 50-yard pitch. It's known as the "hated half-wedge" and even good players struggle with it. Most players would rather face a full wedge shot than one from this distance, because the shorter swing is actually more difficult to control. They find partial swings to be difficult in terms of finding the right rhythm and determining exactly how long a swing they should

You need precise club-ball contact on this shot, and you should eliminate as many moving parts as necessary. On the downswing, concentrate solely on swinging your arms through the ball aggressively. Don't think about your hands at all—your wrists will unload the club naturally through impact. Remember, you do not need to fear hitting the ball too far, provided you've opened the clubface sufficiently during the four-step procedure and curbed the length of your backswing. At all costs, you must really go after the ball through impact, making sure you accelerate your arms. Nothing slows down here—not your arms, hands, or especially, the club.

make. It's a shot that requires a great deal of precision, and there's often a lot of pressure connected to it because of the opportunity to pick up strokes or else save them. The half-wedge comes into play often, usually as a routine third shot on a par 5, or the third shot on a par 4 after a wayward drive. If you become deadly from this tricky range—and there's no reason you shouldn't—you will have a huge advantage in competition.

→ KEEP SHAFT ANGLE CONSTANT

DISTANCE CONTROL IS CRITICAL on the 30- to 50-yard pitch, and the speed you swing your arms is not the only factor. You must maintain the integrity of the clubface by making sure the loft is exactly the same at impact as you programmed at address. In the top photo at near right, you can see how the shaft of the club is leaning toward the target just before the clubhead makes contact with the ball. At impact, it's leaning toward the target at the same angle, and even after impact the clubshaft should have that same target-leaning position. That guarantees that the clubface loft is preserved. The last part of the equation is to prevent the clubface from rotating closed. If you roll your wrists on the downswing, the clubface rolls along with them, thereby forcing it to close. When the clubface closes, it also loses loft. The result is a ball that shoots off lower and farther than you intended when you planned the shot.

MAKE A THIN, SHALLOW DIVOT

On the longer pitch shot, the clubhead should approach the ball on a shallow angle (*top*), the club nevertheless moving downward. The divot that results should be shallow (*bottom*) and reflect the angle of attack.

PLENTY OF SPEED, NO "RELEASE"

Well into the follow-through, the clubface is aimed at the sky, a sign that I haven't released the club by rolling my hands. I've kept my hands quiet and controlled the distance of the shot by how fast I swung my arms.

FINISH IS LONGER THAN BACKSWING

Although I purposely limited the length of my backswing, there is no limit to the length of the follow-through. It always should exceed the length of the backswing. It's a sure sign that you accelerated through the ball.

SHORT SHOT, TOO LONG A BACKSWING

In the photo at right I'm playing a 30-yard pitch. My backswing is much too long for a shot of that length. It has too many moving parts, including too much shoulder rotation and movement in my feet, knees, and hips. All that motion is unnecessary and shrinks the margin for error. Mechanically, the swing is fine—for a 50-yard shot. The chipping motion should be much smaller.

→ AVOID MAKING SWING TOO LONG

GIVEN A CHOICE, I'D RATHER see a backswing that is too short than too long. If your arm swing is too short, you can at least atone for it by hinging your wrists more and applying a little extra acceleration on the downswing. With the long backswing, you're trapped into making two types of downswing. The first is a lazy downswing in which you ease the club into the ball, causing indifferent contact. The other option is even worse—the dreaded "decel" where the club travels slower at impact than it did earlier in the downswing. Decelerating is probably the worst error you can make in chipping (or the full swing for that matter), because it completely disrupts your mechanics. It leads to a lot of fat and thin shots, poor distance and direction control, and every other bad shot in the book.

THE HIGH COST OF DECELERATING

The main purpose of the backswing is to create and store energy. If your backswing is too long, you're creating energy that ultimately has no place to go. On the downswing, you respond by slowing down your hands or stopping them completely. At that point, the wrists unhinge and the club is released into the ground well behind the ball. Result: A fat, "chunked" shot that comes up way short of the hole—if it reaches the green at all. A sure sign of an overly long backswing and deceleration is the club passing the hands (*left* and *inset*). It's one of the most common errors in golf, and a preventable one.

→ LESSONS
IN ACTION

❯

This chip during the CA Championship definitely was from a tight lie. Here, I'm applying quite a bit of clubhead speed for a short shot and making sure I contact the ball first and *then* take the divot. My lower body action, combined with the extension in my arms, is further proof of an accelerating swing.

❮

Even short pitches can require a little extra clubhead speed. This pitch at the 2009 Northern Trust needed a little extra effort, because my ball was sitting down and I needed to make sure the clubhead didn't lose momentum as it plowed through the turf. Notice how my trailing arm has straightened completely. That's a sign of an aggressive move through impact. The shot came off well; my eyes are tracking the flight of the ball.

❯

The absence of a divot on this 35-yard pitch indicates I picked the ball cleanly off the turf rather than deliver a sharp, downward blow. This type of shot is designed to have enough backspin to stop the ball close to where it landed, but not so much that it spins backward far short of the hole. One of the advantages of the hinge-and-hold technique is that it enables you to control spin.

❮

Sometimes I don't wear
a glove when playing
short pitches. It's a
remnant from when
I was a kid and didn't
bother going to all the
trouble of putting on a
glove. Today, I sometimes
put on the glove and
other times don't—it's all
a matter of how I feel
at the moment.

"The flop shot results from an imperfect impact condition. In most cases the clubhead makes contact either behind the ball or directly beneath it."

183

The low, spinning lob is an invaluable weapon
when your lie is somewhat less than perfect
and you have a little green to work with.

→ SECTION V
Flop & Lob

I CHIPPED FOR HOURS IN MY BACKYARD AS A KID
but at some point I'd get a little tired of that, so to have
some fun I'd hit flop and lob shots. What I call a flop
shot is one out of a fluffy lie in the rough where you
don't catch the ball cleanly; it comes out without spin,
so you use trajectory to control the distance and how
softly it lands. A lob is like a flop but out of a lie where
you don't get grass between the club and the ball and
it comes out with spin. They're still fun shots for me to
hit, even though, instead of my no-pressure backyard,
they come when a good score—maybe even the
tournament—is on the line. ›

I STARTED THE FINAL ROUND of the 2002 Bob Hope Chrysler Classic in a tie for 10th place, four shots behind the leader at the PGA West Palmer Course. After birdies on 16 and 17, I needed one more just to get into a playoff, but my approach to 18 found fluffy rough short and left of the green. There was a severe downslope I had to fly over, to get the ball stopped by the hole. To hit the flop, I opened up the face, threw it as high as I could to get it to land as soft as it could, and ended up making the short birdie putt.

Now, granted, sometimes there's luck involved with flop shots, especially if they're short ones, because they must be hit firmly. But if I have a lot of green to work with and the shot won't have spin on it, I can read the green to gauge where I want it to land and how far it'll run. On a lob shot, I generally have much more control, because I'm confident I can hit my spot and, with spin, get the ball to end up at least inside my three-foot putting circle.

• • •

MY BALL-STRIKING WAS A real struggle all week at the 2006 U.S. Open. Halfway through the third round, I was coming off two straight bogeys after missing both fairways and greens and was five shots behind the leaders. Then my drive to the par 3 10th hit close to the front-right pin that was perched on the edge of a downslope but trickled back off the green. Another bogey there and it may have been a real battle just to get into contention with only 26 holes left to play. I pulled the 64-degree wedge to hit a full lob shot over the bunker off a tight lie and got it to stop where it landed, within a foot, and saved a much-needed par.

There were two very different lies there, one in the fluffy stuff, one sitting tight, but both shots were taken under extreme pressure. It's been said that a lot of times it can be tough to two-putt when that's all you're trying to do. This is one reason I take an aggressive approach on most reasonable putts and short shots around the green, even lobs and some flops. I'm thinking "in," on most of them.

• • •

TOUGH OR TIGHT LIES DON'T bother me too much, because I've been working on this area for many years. But there's another reason, too. I see all sorts of players working on their short games giving themselves preferred lies, whether they're chipping or pitching. When practicing, I hit balls from where they lie, whether they're in good lies or not. This gives me a wider variety of practice shots. In a tournament, I may not be happy with a lie, but I've probably seen it before and figured out how to negotiate it.

That final birdie set up by a flop from the rough at the Hope Classic gave me the low score of the day, a 64, and got me into a playoff, which I won, my 20th career win.

Saturday's par on 10 at the Open turned the day and week around. I didn't miss another green in that round, made two birdies, and ended up with a share of the lead heading into the final round. That didn't end so well, but if not for my short game that week, I wouldn't have had a chance.

The flop requires more clubhead speed than usual in order to prevent the turf from slowing down the clubhead.

→ WHICH FLOP OR LOB DO YOU CHOOSE?

FLOPS AND LOBS APPEAR similar, in that you're making a swing that looks to be very long for the short distance you're flying the ball. But there are many nuances in technique that actually place the shots into three distinct categories. The type of flop or lob you play is determined first and foremost by your lie–whether the ball is sitting down in tall grass, suspended in tall grass, or is on hardpan or a tightly mown area near the green. Depending on the quality of your lie, you stop the ball on the green either by spinning it or hitting the ball so high that it can't roll very far after landing. The flop and the lob vary in terms of your ball position, how much you open the clubface, and how cleanly you make contact. The two flop shots shown result from deliberately hitting well behind the ball, while the lob shot results from hitting down steeply on the ball and minimizing how much grass intervenes between the ball and clubface.

FLOP NO. 1: MAKE THE GROUND WORK FOR YOU

The first type of flop occurs when the ground is very firm, with the ball in a tight lie but otherwise sitting well. On this shot, you open the face of your sand wedge and purposely hit a few inches behind the ball. Because you make an aggressive swing, the sole of the clubhead penetrates the firm surface and then deflects off. The clubface makes contact with the ball while traveling upward, resulting in a towering shot that stops quickly after landing. This type of flop is very useful when trying to get the ball close to a hole cut near the edge of the green.

FLOP NO. 2: A CASE FOR MAXIMUM FORCE

The second type of flop is one where you have a very poor lie, with the ball nestled deep in tall grass. Even in the best of circumstances it's hard to tell exactly how the ball will behave, but still you can hit the ball higher and make it land more softly than most golfers imagine. The key is to hit down steeply a couple of inches behind the ball, the clubhead bottoming out directly beneath it.

LOW-SPIN LOB: WORKS FOR FLUFFY LIE

The low-spin lob is the shot to play when you have a fluffy lie, the ball neither sitting cleanly, nor buried so deeply that the ball touches the ground. The goal is to prevent the clubhead from penetrating the grass so deeply before impact that it passes under the ball completely and you hit the ball only a couple of feet. The correct lob technique will produce excellent contact.

→ TIGHT LIE: UNIQUE IMPACT

ONE RULE OF IRON PLAY is that the clubhead must be traveling downward at impact if you are to get the ball airborne. There is one exception to that rule: when your ball is sitting on hardpan or a tight fairway lie with firm ground beneath the ball. This is one iron shot where you actually will hit the ball on the upswing, the clubhead traveling upward at the moment of impact. At first glance that seems impossible; with no "cushion" or soft area beneath the ball, how can the club possibly be moving upward at impact? In fact, not only can you make it happen, you can do it with ease.

The challenge is mainly conceptual. Your goal is to make the clubhead penetrate that hard ground behind the ball, and let it continue down and forward until the resistance from the ground causes the clubface to bounce upward into the ball. The ball comes out very high and lands softly.

ANOTHER ONE-FOOT TEST

Remember the one-foot test for the downhill lie in sand? The same thing applies here. You need to position your weight almost completely on your front foot, the ball positioned well forward in your stance, to promote a very steep angle of approach on the downswing. Lay the clubface wide open, so that it's almost flat, with the top of the toe of the clubhead nearly touching the ground.

CLUBHEAD TRAVELING UPWARD: SEEING IS BELIEVING

In the sequence above, the tee in the ground adjacent to the ball helps demonstrate the unusual impact condition of the flop from a tight lie. The clubface is wide open at address (A), both to provide loft and to expose the bounce along the sole. The clubhead contacts the ground a few inches behind the ball, then ricochets upward into the base of the ball (B), sending it flying at a near-vertical angle. The divot (*large photo*) reveals the speed and force necessary to pull off the shot.

TIGHT LIE

→ GIVE IT ALL YOU'VE GOT

FLOPS AND LOBS REQUIRE a lot of swing speed. The extreme loft you attain by opening the clubface is the primary reason; in addition to height, you need enough power to make the ball go forward. With the flop from a tight lie, you have the added challenge of making the clubhead penetrate a firm surface and continue moving forward after it digs into the ground. You can't afford to let resistance from the ground slow the clubhead; it must keep moving toward the target. So you need to make a full backswing, one in which the range of motion is as great as with a full iron shot. The hinge-and-hold technique is another imperative. Your hands must lead the way throughout the downswing, and you want to generate as much speed as possible with your arms. You don't need to fear making such a large swing, however, as there actually is a pretty wide margin for error on this type of flop shot. You can make contact with the ground a little forward or behind the point you were aiming for and still get a decent result, thanks to the sole of the club rebounding after it penetrates the ground.

(A)

MAKE AN ALL-OUT BACKSWING

A short backswing won't work on the flop from a tight lie, because the length of the swing won't permit you to generate enough speed with your arms on the downswing. Go ahead and make a full turn with your shoulders and hips (A).

B

C

DOWNSWING: POUR ON THE POWER

Your downswing should be as aggressive as possible without losing your balance (B). Make sure your weight is on your forward foot as you accelerate your arms. You want your hands to approach the ball on a steep angle.

LET THE SPEED CARRY YOU INTO A HIGH FINISH

Although the ground will offer some resistance through impact, concentrate hard on building so much acceleration that *nothing* can slow your clubhead through impact. The fuller the follow-through, the better your chances of succeeding (C).

→ POOR LIE: THE ULTIMATE FLOP-SHOT CHALLENGE

IF THERE'S A SITUATION THAT'S A DISASTER in the making for players of all levels, it's the ball buried deep in thick greenside rough. It's especially discouraging when you've "short-sided" yourself–missed the green on the same side where the hole is located, leaving you little green to work with. The truth is, getting the ball within three feet of the hole consistently will always be a challenge because every lie is a little different. But this situation is far from hopeless; there is a type of flop shot that will give you a reasonable chance at making par. The flop from a poor lie has one limitation: You can't apply any backspin at all due to so much grass intervening between the ball and clubface. There is only one way to make the ball settle quickly after landing, and that's to hit the ball very high. If you get the ball up quickly on a steep, upward trajectory, it will land on the green at an acute angle and come to a quick stop.

A QUESTION OF DEPTH

My lie in the photo below is a poor one, and typical of what happens when you miss a green by only a few yards. It's obvious that a chipping motion won't produce enough clubhead speed, while a routine pitch won't hit the ball high enough to make it come to a quick stop. I've begun the process by opening the clubface and aiming behind the ball. If the grass were taller and the ball sitting worse, I'd open the face even more.

HOW STEEP A SWING DO YOU NEED?

I've opened the clubface to an extreme and aimed a few inches behind the ball (*inset*). You need a lot of swing speed for this type of flop along with a steep angle of approach. Thus, I've hinged my wrists fully and swung my lead arm back a good distance while allowing my shoulders to turn. The face of my 60-degree wedge is fanned wide open. I'm carrying only one image in my mind at this point. It's an image of the clubhead penetrating the grass behind the ball on a sharp downward angle, so the clubhead reaches the lowest point of its arc directly beneath the ball. Notice that my weight is predominantly on my forward foot.

/ 195 /

DON'T GET CUTE—SWING DOWN WITH PLENTY OF FORCE

On the flop from thick rough, I typically make a swing that, in normal circumstances, would produce a shot of about 90 yards—my maximum distance with the 60-degree sand wedge. But due to the poor lie, the open position of the clubface, and the indirect contact I'm making, the ball will fly only 15 feet. You must have an aggressive mindset and execute the shot aggressively, too, using as much arm speed as you can generate. All of your swing energy should be directed downward, your weight remaining on your forward foot as you drive your hands into a low finish. When the clubhead reaches the bottom of its arc, the ball will pop up at a very sharp angle (*right*), with almost no spin.

POOR LIE

→ TIME TO FORCE THE ISSUE

THE BIGGEST DANGER ON THE FLOP from a nasty lie is allowing the grass to grab the clubhead and slow it down before it reaches the lowest point of its arc. Another possibility is the grass wrapping around the hosel of the clubhead and twisting the clubface closed, which will decrease the loft you absolutely must have to attain the high trajectory you need. When you play this shot, keep in mind that it involves more force than

EXPECT RESISTANCE, ABBREVIATED FINISH

Because you're attacking the ball on such a steep angle, the clubhead may very well be brought to a sudden stop after it bottoms out beneath the ball. That's fine; it shows you delivered the clubhead into impact correctly. You can see to what extreme I opened the clubface (*opposite*), and how I fought to keep it open through impact (*left*). If you can maintain that open clubface, the shot will come off as planned—high and lazy, with a "dead" landing when it hits the green. Take a close look at my eyes and how they are following the flight of the ball. They pretty much give away the fact I've flopped the ball on a very high trajectory.

finesse. You have to exert a lot of clubhead speed and also some strength. Grip the club more firmly than usual, and keep your wrists solid as the clubhead travels through impact. This is where the hinge-and-hold technique really helps, because it prevents you from getting too handsy and throwing the clubhead into the ground. Lead with your arms and hands, and anticipate resistance from the turf at impact.

→ PERFECT LIE? EXECUTE THE LOW, SPINNING LOB

NOW THAT WE'VE COVERED THE FLOP from a tight lie and a poor lie, what about the classic good lie with the ball sitting up perfectly? Obviously you have a great deal of flexibility and can play any type of shot you like. But a neat shot that is tailor-made for the good lie is the low, spinning lob. It's a nice shot to have in your repertoire, especially when you have a fair amount of green to work with, want to hit the ball low, but also need it to brake to a halt after it lands. This is a cool shot to watch and an even cooler one to execute, because it demands a little creativity. The goal is to create what I call a "splicing" impact condition, where the clubface moves down sharply and catches the ball cleanly. Although you don't accelerate into the ball with lots of speed, it nevertheless comes out with a lot of backspin and stops very quickly.

KEY IS TECHNIQUE, NOT PURE FORCE

To play the low, spinning lob, open the clubface generously with the ball a shade farther back in your stance than normal to promote a steep angle of approach. Use the hinge-and-hold technique, keeping your backswing relatively short. Because you're anticipating clean club-ball contact, you don't need a great deal of clubhead speed. You're planning for a low trajectory, the ball loaded with backspin despite the fact that you aren't hitting it very hard.

A PERFECT LIE, RIPE FOR THE LOW LOB

This lie is a dream come true for every golfer, and I have to say, I get a little excited just finding my ball in a position like this. There is no chance of grass getting between the ball and clubface, nor is the lie so tight that it forces me to play a full-blooded flop. With a lie this good, you can play any shot you like, but preferably one where the clubface meets the ball cleanly before continuing down to take a divot.

OPEN CLUBFACE AND A STEEP APPROACH

On the downswing, think only of accelerating, maintaining the hinge in your wrist, and striking the ball cleanly. Your angle of approach is steep and the clubface remains open. Through impact, the clubface will shave the surface of the ball, the sharp edges of the grooves grabbing the ball's soft cover and imparting a tremendous amount of spin (*right*). Remember, you are creating backspin not by generating a tremendous amount of clubhead speed, but by the quality of your impact. As always, avoid applying a sudden burst of speed with your hands as the clubhead approaches the ball. If you unhinge your wrists, you won't get that neat splicing action through impact, and you'll wind up with an ordinary shot that doesn't check up after landing on the green.

SPINNING LOB

→ A "SPLICING" IMPACT CONDITION

SAVE FOR THE FEW OCCASIONS when you deliberately hit behind the ball, the low, spinning lob is the only iron shot you'll hit where you aren't trying to compress the ball as fully and efficiently as possible. Instead of trying to squash the ball against the clubface, the goal is to make the ball skim across the surface, so there's a lot of friction and the cover of the ball is grabbed by the grooves of your sand wedge. The action is a

Although you're delivering a downward blow, the clubhead does not penetrate down so far that you take a big divot. As there is not much resistance from the turf, you should continue into a free follow-through, with both arms extended in the classic "hold" portion of the hinge-and-hold technique (*left*). Note that my follow-through isn't especially long; it should mirror the backswing—short and crisp, with the hands leading the way. The ball has come out low, but not necessarily fast. Expect it to float onto the green and bite on the third bounce, trickling a short way to the hole after that.

little similar to a shot in table tennis where you try to impart a backspin—you do it by knifing down and through with your paddle while maintaining loft. This shot behaves true to its name; it starts out on a low trajectory and appears as though it will run after it hits the green, but instead checks and then rolls only a short distance. It's a great weapon when your lie isn't perfect and you don't have much green to work with.

I CALL IT "NEGATIVE LOFT"

Only accomplished players should try the backward shot, as it requires good balance and excellent hand-eye coordination to pull off successfully (and safely!). Address the ball with your upper body perpendicular to the upslope, almost all of your weight on your rear foot. Looking down, you'll notice the face of the club has so much loft it actually is aimed behind you (*large photo, right*). Make a full, deliberate backswing (*inset*), turning your shoulders as far as you humanly can while keeping your lower body quiet.

→ LET'S HAVE SOME FUN

IF THERE'S A SHOT I've enjoyed more than any other over the years, it's the backward shot that flies in the opposite direction of where I'm aiming. In the sequence of photos at right, the ball ends up coming down very close to where the photographer is standing. After I learned to play the shot as a kid, I longed for the day when I could use it in tournament play. The odds of it happening were rare; the ball needs to be perched on a severe uphill lie, a rare predicament to say the least. But at long last I got my chance during an AT&T Pebble Beach Pro-Am. The gallery had to wonder what I was up to when I addressed the ball facing away from the green. But when the shot came off as planned and landed on the green, the gallery went wild. And so did I.

RADICAL SWING FOR A RADICAL SHOT

On the forward swing, keep your weight on your rear foot. Swing your arms as fast as possible and allow your wrists to unhinge early—the only time in this book I've suggested you release the club early! Do not roll your wrists over. Instead, cup the wrist of your gloved hand so the face is aimed at the target behind you. The ball will fly backward over your shoulder (*left* and *inset*). When the ball hits the green, you'll witness something bizarre. The ball will zip even farther away from you, the result of pure topspin. The shot is a blast to pull off, and why not? Fun is what this game is all about.

→ LESSONS
IN ACTION

❯

This is a high flop from a dicey greenside lie during the 2008 U.S. Open at Torrey Pines. The greens were running quick, and a standard chip that landed on the green would have run well past the hole. I made a very aggressive swing; notice that my shoulders have unwound completely and that the heel of my rear foot has come off the ground.

❮

I remember this shot from the 2009 CA Championship very well. My ball was perched up so high, I feared the clubhead would travel under the ball. So, I rolled my wrists over so the clubface would be square at impact rather than open. It was one of the rare instances where my clubhead finished in a toe-up position on the follow-through.

❯

Here's another photo taken during the 2008 U.S. Open. I'm playing a low, spinning lob, the ball flying only slightly above head height. While my lie was good, I still chose the low, spinning lob technique I explained earlier in this section. Notice that my trailing arm has straightened, and I've directed my hands up the line of play, toward the target.

Everyone, myself
included, is craning
their necks to follow
the flight of this flop
shot, played during the
final round of the 2009
CA Championship. This
was a full-blooded flop
in which I swung with
practically all the speed
and power I possess.
Doral Country Club, site
of the tournament, has
Bermuda grass, and if the
ball is sitting down, you
really have to accelerate
to hit the ball high.

Acknowledgments

EVERYTHING IN THIS BOOK came out of the backyard practice area my father built. He taught me and my brother and sister there and we fell in love with the game there. More than an acknowledgment, I owe him a debt I can never repay. Years ago my manager, Steve Loy, and my friend, Terry Jastrow, started talking to me about doing an instructional DVD and book. I thank them for their foresight and their patience and making those projects a reality. Guy Yocom and T.R. Reinman have been writing about me for almost 25 years and once again did a great job bringing my voice to print. I have been associated with *Golf Digest* since I turned pro and would like to thank my friend and Editor-in-Chief, Jerry Tarde, as well as his entire staff for their unending generosity and attention to detail. Dom Furore and J.D. Cuban are two of the very best golf photographers working today and did their best work for this project. The book's designer, Tim Oliver, did much to organize the photography as well as the text, and really made it shine. The team at HarperCollins also worked tirelessly to make the book one I am truly proud of. To all of you, a heartfelt thanks for your dedication to your craft and mine.